Hiking Waterfalls Hawai'i

A Guide to the State's Best Waterfall Hikes

Justin A. Brackett

FALCONGUIDES

ESSEX, CONNECTICUT

FALCONGUIDES®

An imprint of Globe Pequot, the trade division of
The Rowman & Littlefield Publishing Group, Inc.
4501 Forbes Blvd., Ste. 200
Lanham, MD 20706
www.rowman.com

Falcon and FalconGuides are registered trademarks and Make Adventure Your Story is a trademark of The Rowman & Littlefield Publishing Group, Inc.

Distributed by NATIONAL BOOK NETWORK

Photos by Justin A. Brackett unless otherwise noted
Maps by Hugh Mullen III and The Rowman & Littlefield Publishing Group, Inc.

British Library Cataloguing in Publication Information available

Library of Congress Cataloging-in-Publication Data
Names: Brackett, Justin, author.
Title: Hiking waterfalls Hawaii : a guide to the state's best waterfall hikes / Justin A. Brackett.
Description: Guilford, Connecticut : FalconGuides, 2022. | Includes bibliographical references and
    index. | Summary: "A guide to the best waterfall hikes in Hawaii, through state and national parks,
    forests, monuments and wilderness areas, and from popular city parks to the most remote and
    secluded corners of the state"— Provided by publisher.
Identifiers: LCCN 2022000019 (print) | LCCN 2022000020 (ebook) | ISBN 9781493055791
    (paperback) | ISBN 9781493055807 (epub)
Subjects: LCSH: Hiking—Hawaii—Guidebooks. | Trails—Hawaii—Guidebooks. | Waterfalls—
    Hawaii—Guidebooks. | Hawaii—Guidebooks.
Classification: LCC GV199.42.H3 B73 2022 (print) | LCC GV199.42.H3 (ebook) |
    DDC 796.5109969—dc23/eng/20220104
LC record available at https://lccn.loc.gov/2022000019
LC ebook record available at https://lccn.loc.gov/2022000020

The author and The Rowman & Littlefield Publishing Group, Inc., assume no liability for accidents happening to, or injuries sustained by, readers who engage in the activities described in this book.

Visit these trails at your own risk with respect and great care. Do not trespass. Make sure to hike within your ability and stay on the trail. When in doubt, stay out. If the water is brown, turn around, don't drown. The information included in this book is current as of October 2021 and may change with time. Make sure to research the current status of access. Check the weather before every adventure.

To every wide-eyed dreamer of Hawai'i, whether you've been blessed to grace her shores or only came as close as daydreaming of her by pulling up surfcam live feeds while sitting at a desk in your office eating a sack lunch.

The word *Hawai'i* evokes images of teal seas lapping against half-moon sandy bay beaches. It also brings one's eyes up from the seas to the sheer, jagged cliffs, which appear to rise immediately behind the beaches. Clouds, high atop the mountains above, pour rainwater that has been carried across thousands of miles of the Pacific Ocean into the deep gulches. These canyons hold within them cascading waters seemingly falling from the heavens that support diverse, oftentimes endemic, species within their tropical rainforests.

This book takes you into Hawai'i's mountains and deep into her valleys to the headwalls, where you can find those waterfalls you dream of. They are waiting for you. Get in here to get out there.

Overview

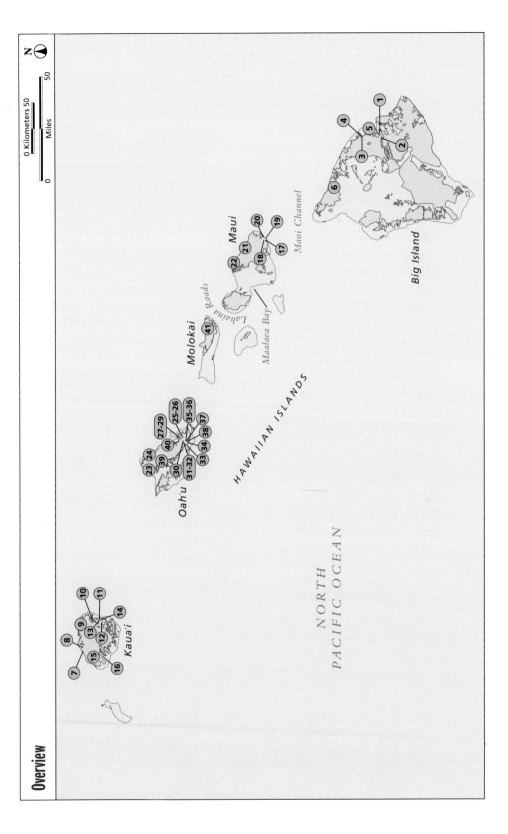

0 Kilometers 50

0 Miles 50

N

Kauaʻi

Oahu

Molokai

Maui

Big Island

NORTH
PACIFIC OCEAN

HAWAIIAN ISLANDS

Lahaina Roads

Maalaea Bay

Maui Channel

Contents

The Hikes

Acknowledgments

This book is dedicated to the beautiful people of Hawai'i. You took me in, shared your gorgeous mountains and valleys with me, and provided me a family of adventurers to grow with. That *ohana* made this book possible.

To those who walked the trails with me. To those who invited me to hike to places I had never been before. To those who shared their excitement for preserving and respecting this land. To those who taught me the names of ridges, valleys, and the rare and exotic plants and wildlife of Hawai'i. You made this book possible.

Hawai'i is full of trails that have been traveled for centuries. The love of adventure, preservation, and education continues to inspire so many of us to give back and foster an appreciation for our trails. My hope is that this book, and all that I do here, brings a positive energy and more love to Hawai'i's hiking and conservation community.

Whether you are 8 or 80, lacing up your boots and hitting the trails will nurture your soul. Feel the sweat running down your brow, your heartbeat pumping strong, and the heat of the sun on your face as you make your way to that sacred spot you dreamt about. Breathe the fresh air, feel the soft water drops fall onto your bare skin, and awaken your entire body as you dive into the freezing cold pools and become one with the *'aina*.

Immerse yourself in the outdoors and let it take you, as it has taken me, to an appreciation for this beautiful Earth we get to call home. To our Creator be the glory. May we always protect what You have made for us.

Meet Your Guide

Justin A. Brackett first ventured to Hawai'i in 1998 with his family for a ten-day vacation. His mother, Nancy Brackett, and his grandmother, Grace Hawkins, held a deep appreciation for the islands. After six trips from Tennessee, he made lucky number seven a one-way ticket, sold everything he owned, and arrived in Honolulu with three suitcases.

Justin is the owner of Hawai'i's largest hiking store: Uloha at 515 Ward Avenue, Honolulu. Uloha enables him to shine a light on the various nonprofit organizations that preserve Hawai'i's flora and fauna, protect the sacred cultural sites, and clean and maintain the many, many trails. Uloha stands for "Uncle's Local Outfitter of Hawai'i Adventures" since Justin is a proud uncle of eight nieces and nephews and four greatnieces. The store was started in order to bring a positive light to hiking in Hawai'i and to help keep those who travel its trails safe.

Justin is a founding member of O'ahu Search and Rescue, a nonprofit SAR team dedicated to wilderness search and rescue. With the motto of "May they always come home," OSAR works to bring home those who go missing in Hawai'i's mountains and valleys. Although Hawai'i doesn't have poisonous snakes or ferocious bears, the trails here are often overgrown and the jagged cliffs can be very treacherous.

Justin graduated from the University of Tennessee in 2001 and from Chicago-Kent College of Law in 2005. As an attorney, he practices consumer protection law, helping the people of Hawai'i right the wrongs that happen to them. Just as one who bears the torch lights the way for those around them, Justin believes in carrying a positive light throughout the world. As your guide, he hopes to instill in you a deep appreciation and reverence for the islands he now calls home.

Introduction

This is a story of hope, a story of pain, and a story of perseverance. People flock to the isles of Hawai'i for two majestic beauties: her beaches and her mountains. They desire to feel the warm sand between their toes and stand in awe of the crystal-clear cool mountain water cascading to white down her many, many waterfalls.

I too came in search of these, the staples of a perfect Hawaiian escape. I came to run the ridges and chase the waterfalls. I came to be at one with a land so perfect, so pristine, so bountiful . . . it could be Eden. I longed to sit in a wilderness with nothing but the birds singing, the brooks babbling, and the sun warming my face; to follow the streams to the headwall and swim below a cliff face that stands towering hundreds of feet above me.

These idyllic moments can still be found, but are becoming more and more rare as hordes of tourists, around ten million each year, make their way to find their Hawai'i experience. No one can fault them, especially not one who shared their vision not so long ago.

But their arrival, and their search for Eden, is costing Hawai'i a lot. Their tramping through her jungles, across her deserts, and even in her cities wears her down. It makes her weak, introducing invasive species that overpower her native children. It leads to wider and wider paths when they strive to keep their white tennis shoes clean on her unkept muddy trails. It causes runoff of her soils into the ocean at an alarming rate. It tramples the majestic beauty we all seek to find until it is no longer recognizable, or even suitable for human consumption.

This book is written to bring awareness to her plight. To remind us all that we do not own, and can never own, Hawai'i. She is wild. She is free. She was here before us and will be long after we are all gone. When confronted by outside invaders, the Hawaiian people gave up their claims to her, as she was never theirs, or ours, in the first place.

Hawai'i was, and is still, another member of our family. A mother that provides all we need. One that can teach us how to be better versions of ourselves. If we care for her, she will care for us. If we neglect or turn our backs on her, she will continue on, but we will be the ones losing out on her loving embrace and nurturing heart.

May we all love our Mother Earth. May we come together to respect her in front of all of our friends. May we leave her in a better state than that which we found her. Together we can build up her trails so they carry visitors to her beautiful hidden gems without causing damage in the process. The visitors will come in search of their Eden. Let us all preserve her for generations to come to experience their awe, gain their inspiration, and learn to respect, not own, the one who nurtures us all.

There were around one million native Hawaiians living in this, the most remote island chain in the world, when explorers arrived in the 1700s. They were entirely self-sufficient and prosperous. Today there are about the same number of residents,

but residents import over 90 percent of what we consume. How could this happen in such a rich environment? A combination of factors contributed to us getting to such a place of dependence, the largest of which is our forgetting the natives' systems of caring for the *'aina* (land) and *ala* (water).

Native Hawaiian steppe systems of *loi* (taro patches) stretching from high in the *mauka* (mountains) down to the *makai* (ocean), understanding of the trade winds, and *loko i'a kuapā* (fish ponds) increased the crop yields and fish production. They kept invasive plants at bay, introduced no toxins to the soil or rivers, and divided each island into a genius *ahupua'a* (self-sustaining tribes) system. We have lots to learn from them. May their traditions be remembered and their love for these islands be renewed through us.

With some of the wettest spots on earth, Hawai'i is chock-full of waterfalls. Every ridge gives way to a valley, and every valley holds a streambed that charges up with tropical rain showers dumping some of the cleanest water in the world onto the mountain summits above. Rains cross over 2,000 miles of open ocean no matter which way they came from. Falling to the sea, blowing or evaporating back into clouds, then falling to the sea again . . . over and over and over again as they make their way to the sheer mountain peaks of Hawai'i's islands. Some of those peaks rise to over 13,800 feet from the ocean surface to form massive impediments for the trade winds and Pacific Ocean storms, resulting in the constant watering of this oasis on the most remote island chain in the world. Hawai'i welcomes you to come respectfully and experience it for yourself.

This book will help you find your way to some of the most remote and pristine landscapes on the planet. Understand that Hawai'i's jagged mountains were not as exploited as some on the mainland. There are not many nineteenth-century or even twentieth-century mining, logging, or forest service roads. The trails were oftentimes cut by sugarcane plantation workers hired to divert the water from waterfalls or streams to their fields, or hiking "trampers" who explored deep into the valleys and told others of the waterfalls they found.

Trails often follow ridgelines, water drainages, or ungulate (such as pig, goat, or cattle) paths. They are rugged, with lots of slick roots, mud, and rocks. Oftentimes they are not well-defined and poorly marked. I may encourage you to look for the "elephant trail," which is the trail that most appears as though a herd of elephants has recently traveled along it. Remember that you can always turn around if you feel as though you are off-trail.

Make sure to wear shoes with deep, spread-apart lugs that will grip in deep mud and shed the mud so it doesn't just cake on them. If you don't have deep-lugged boots or want extra stability on Hawai'i's slick trails, you may want to supplement with some shoe spikes, which are like small crampons used to keep you from sliding in icy conditions.

Being near the equator and in the middle of the Pacific Ocean, it is often hot, humid, and/or rainy while hiking in Hawai'i. So, check the weather and always be prepared with the Essentials of Wilderness Travel (see the "Before You Hit the Trail" section below) before you drive to the trailhead. Understand that the weather can be very different in the mountains than it is in Waikiki. Expect it to change rapidly at any time while you hike, especially near the streams or summits. Most rescues can be avoided with proper preparation and realistic expectations. Study the length of the trail and elevation change, then plan your hike around the heat of the day.

Work together with your hiking companions to watch out for each other. Don't ever feel like you can't ask for a break when you need one. I've seen many uncles, aunties, grandparents, and so forth let themselves get overheated or winded by chasing after their younger loved ones. Use excuses such as tying your shoe, taking a photo, or observing some pretty plant to slow them down and help them see the little things they might miss by going too fast.

Hiking is so liberating. Anyone can do it. All it takes is putting one foot in front of the other over and over until you reach your destination. But remember that once you reach your destination, you are typically only halfway through your hike. You should save enough energy and supplies to get all the way back to the trailhead and your transportation back home. And make sure to leave early enough so you have sufficient daylight to get back out.

I say much of this because hiker rescues are an all too common topic on Hawai'i's nightly news. Many of those rescues are preventable. Some are not. People should be able to call for help when they need it, but the system is said to be getting overwhelmed at times. Charging for rescues is getting way too much discussion. The fire departments and search and rescue teams are opposed to charging for rescues because it may prevent people from calling when they are first in need of help, potentially leading to them getting into even more trouble.

Trails have been shut down due to rescues and neighborhood complaints. Sacred Falls, Mariners Ridge, Kamehame Ridge, and Stairway to Heaven are just a few of the trails that have been closed in the past thirty years. Maunawili Falls, Kuliouou Ridge, and Koko Crater Stairs have recently been complained about by residents of the neighborhoods their trailheads are in. Stairway to Heaven is currently under a giant chopping block, with the City of Honolulu wanting to spend $1 million to have the stairs removed due to the complaints of a few property owners in the back of Haiku Valley.

Hawai'i's trails are under attack! The legislature doesn't fund them adequately to keep them safe. Hawai'i does not invest in new facilities or hiker education programs like it should considering the millions of visitors that hit the trails here every year. It seems the state would rather close a trail than work to improve it. A large budget is being spent to lure more tourists into coming, but a much smaller amount is spent to maintain the beaches and waterfalls they come to see.

Alas, there is hope. Lots of grassroots organizations are rolling up their sleeves and working hard to help. O'ahu Search and Rescue recently teamed up with Hawaiian Airlines to provide hiker safety tips to new visitors. Organizations such as 808 Clean-ups fight hard to keep our trails and beaches clean. Nonprofits like the Hawaiian Trail and Mountain Corporation pick up the slack from the severely underfunded Nā Ala Hele trail system with weekly trail clearing and maintenance events. The Kokonut Koalition recently rebuilt the Koko Crater Tramway. My goal in opening Hawai'i's hiking store, Uloha, and encouraging volunteering as much as possible is to *free the trails* so the people of Hawai'i get to see hiking in a more positive light. Hopefully this book will help keep the momentum growing.

Close your doors quietly, whisper until you get into the woods and away from the homes, don't play your music loud, clean up around trailheads, say hi to the neighbors as you pass them, and show others that hikers are good for Hawai'i. Practice Leave No Trace principles and share them with others. Understand that we are all just passing through. These mountains and streams will outlive us all, and we need to protect and preserve them for generations to come. The city will rise and some buildings will fall, but the waterfalls will still be there, linking us to those who came before and the many that will come after. Please treat them with the respect you give the places you love.

Come with me as I tell you of my adventures into these deep valleys, narrow canyons, sandy coastlines, and winding roads and trails. Start planning your journeys under the thick canopies of Hawai'i's lush rainforests. Let your mind drift away as you picture yourself rock-hopping your way to the headwall or cliff-jumping into a crystal-clear pool. Dream of the days of old, when Native Hawaiians farmed the *ahupua'a*, cultivating terraces of taro from high in the valleys all the way to the sea. This is Hawai'i, and here are forty-one of her best waterfall hikes. I hope you enjoy them as much as I do.

Before You Hit the Trail

Warnings! Safety briefing: What to know before you go.

1. Stay on the trail and *do not* trespass. Many of Hawai'i's trails are on private or state land. Please be courteous and only hike where you are allowed to go.
   a. Permits: Respect the landowners who offer hikers access. Make sure to get a permit wherever necessary. It helps with resources and safety.
2. Check the weather. Only go when the weather is favorable for your activity. Watch for the stream to turn brown to signal a flash flood is starting. *Do not* get caught in a flash flood! Many die when they get overwhelmed by the speed by which the stream can rise.
3. Beware of leptospirosis. *Do not* drink the stream water without first purifying it. *Do not* go swimming in streams with open cuts. This flesh-eating bacteria is deadly.
4. Beware of falling hazards.
   a. Unmaintained trails: Hawai'i's trails are subject to extreme rain and wind and are not maintained as well as trails in other parts of the world.
   b. Slick mud: I suggest buying mini crampons or super-deep lugged shoes.
   c. Falling rocks: Lava rock in Hawai'i is often porous and brittle. It may break under your weight, so test steps before having them bear your weight and call out "ROCK!" to let others know if you pop any rock or dirt loose.
   d. Flash floods: Watch the weather forecast before venturing into any streambed. Know that the weather can change fast, so watch the level of the stream and exit quickly if it starts to rise or turn brown.
5. Practice safe cliff jumping.
   a. Do not jump unless you feel very confident.
   b. Test all pool depths before you jump into them.
   c. The last steps before the edge of a cliff are often slick, so when in doubt just leave it to the professionals.
6. Go prepared.
   a. Before you venture into Hawai'i's wilderness, make sure to have the O'ahu Search and Rescue Essentials of Wilderness Travel:
      i. Extra water
      ii. Extra food
      iii. Tool kit
      iv. Shelter
      v. Extra layers
      vi. Rain jacket
      vii. Flashlight

        viii. Fire starter

        ix. First-aid kit

        x. Map and compass

        xi. Shoe spikes

        xii. Sun protection

    b. Leave all valuables at home. Hawai'i trailheads are notorious for car break-ins.

    c. Make sure to tell someone where you are going and when you expect to return before you go.

    d. Make any requisite reservations well in advance, as Hawai'i tourist attractions can get very busy during peak seasons (e.g., summer and Christmas holidays).

    e. Have a hiking plan before you go, and don't go on a trail that is above your limits.

7. Use caution and follow proper etiquette on the trail.

    a. Watch the time. Know that you are only halfway through your adventure when you arrive at the waterfall. Leave some gas in the tank to hike out. Have a turn-around time if you could possibly wind up hiking near sunset.

    b. Avoid undue risk.

    c. Read all posted signs.

    d. Respect other trail users.

    c. Pack out at least what you pack in.

How to Use This Guide

Overview

This section provides a brief description of each hike, often listing some of its highlights.

Start

This is a short summary of the starting location for the hike.

Distance

The distance specified in each description is listed as a round-trip distance from the trailhead to the end of the route and back unless otherwise noted. As mentioned in the individual hike descriptions, some of the hikes could work well with car shuttles. All hike mileages assume that you are able to start at the trailhead.

Hike lengths have been estimated as closely as possible using topographic maps, government measurements, and GPS units. With state park hikes, the detailed distances noted on each park's trail map were usually used. However, the different sources do not always agree, so the final figure is sometimes the author's best estimate.

Difficulty

Assessing a hike's difficulty can be very subjective. The elevation, elevation change, and length all play a role, as do trail condition, weather, and the hiker's physical condition. However, even my subjective ratings will give some idea of difficulty. To me, elevation change and whether the trail requires climbing while using your hands in addition to your feet were the most significant variables in establishing levels of difficulty. Many of the hikes have only small elevation changes and are rated easy or moderate. A few trails are rated difficult, though, due to their danger and/or elevation change.

In general, if a hike gains less than 1,000 feet and is less than 8 miles round-trip, I would rate it as easy. Within each category there are many degrees of difficulty, of course. Obviously a 2-mile hike gaining 200 feet is going to be much easier than an 8-mile hike gaining 900 feet. Moderate hikes usually gain somewhere between 1,000 and 2,000 feet and run longer than 8 miles. The strenuous hikes usually gain over 2,000 feet and are fairly long.

Hawai'i trails are different, though! Poor trails, excessive heat, stream crossings with lots of rock-hopping, cross-country travel, and other factors may result in a more difficult designation than would otherwise seem to be the case from simply the elevation change and trail length. Some of the trails even involve climbing up or down cliff faces using both your feet and your hands to travel. Stay within your comfort zone and always be willing to turn back around if the conditions get beyond your zone. The waterfall will be there when you want to visit again.

Keep in mind that carrying a heavy backpack can make even an "easy" day hike fairly strenuous.

Hiking Time

The hiking time is a rough estimate of the time it will take the average hiker to complete the hike. Very fit, fast-moving hikers will be able to complete it in less time. Slow-moving hikers or those preoccupied with activities such as photography may take longer. To come up with this information, I estimated that most people hike at 2 to 3 miles per hour. For longer hikes with more elevation changes, I estimated closer to 2 miles per hour. For short, flat hikes, 3 miles per hour is easily attained. I also tried to take into account other factors such as a rough trail or particularly big elevation changes.

Elevation Change

Elevation is generally the most important factor in determining a hike's difficulty. Elevation change (gain or loss) is provided from the trailhead to the waterfall. Often, but not always, the trailhead lies at the low point and the waterfall lies at the highest point. With many hikes, the highest point may occur somewhere along the path, and you may descend to the waterfall. Some of the hikes have several ups and downs on the way, requiring more elevation change and effort than the number indicates. The hikes along the coast or along the side of roads generally have very minimal elevation changes.

The extremely high humidity and low elevations encountered on some of the hikes may require additional effort. Physically fit hikers coming from outside of Hawai'i should acclimate easily within two or three days for the hikes in this book.

Trail Surface

Trail surface describes the material that makes up the trail. Most commonly it is simply a dirt path or streambed consisting of the native materials that were there when the trail was built. On occasion gravel is added or the trail may be paved. In a few instances the hike follows a dirt road or even a paved road. A few are cross-country routes.

Seasons/Schedule

To escape the heat in Hawai'i, go to the higher elevations or pick a hike with a good swimming hole. Winter and spring are the rainy season in Hawai'i but it is still an excellent time to hike, with pleasant temperatures and a variety of wildflowers. The rains slow from July through September but it brings warmer temperatures. Always check weather forecasts before starting your hike.

Some hiking destinations have opening or closing times, such as La'ie Falls or Kapena Falls in the back of the memorial gardens. Unless you are camping, many state parks allow day-use guests in the park only from 6 a.m. to 10 p.m. or similar times.

Fees and Permits

Permits are not usually required to hike in Hawai'i's parks and forests, although some have a small park entry fee. Some of the National Park Service areas and state parks allow only day use on certain trails. Generally, all National Park Service areas and state parks require a permit for overnight trips. In most areas a fee is required for overnight camping.

Land Status

The land status simply tells which agency, usually federal or state, manages the land in which the trail lies. In this book the Hawai'i Department of Land and Natural Resources (DLNR), USDA Forest Service, and the National Park Service are the most common land managers.

Nearest Town

The nearest town is the closest city or town to the hike's trailhead that has at least minimal visitor services. The listed town will usually have gas, food, and lodging available. In small towns and villages, the hours these services are available may be limited.

Other Trail Users

This describes the other users that you might encounter on the hike. Mountain bikers, hunters, and equestrians are the most common.

Canine Compatibility

This section describes whether dogs are allowed on the trail. Generally dogs need to be leashed when they are allowed. Please be courteous and pick up after your pet.

Water Availability

Sources of water are listed if they are known to usually be reliable. Any water obtained on a hike should be purified before use. Be sure to check about the status of water sources before depending on them. Droughts, livestock and wildlife use, and other factors can change their status.

Finding the Trailhead

This section provides detailed directions to the trailhead. With a basic current state highway map or GPS unit, you can easily locate the starting point from the directions. In general, the nearest town is used as the starting point.

Distances were usually measured using Google Maps or a car odometer. Realize that different cars and different apps will vary slightly in their measurements. Even the same car will read slightly differently driving uphill versus downhill on a dirt road. Be sure to keep an eye open for the specific signs, junctions, and landmarks mentioned in the directions, not just the mileages. The map services available on cell phone GPS systems are often inaccurate or nonexistent in remote areas, so use them with care. In addition, many require decent cell service to work, further lessening their value.

Most of this guide's hikes have trailheads that can be reached by a sedan. Hawai'i's rains can temporarily make some roads impassable. Before venturing onto unimproved dirt roads, you should check with park or forest headquarters. On less-traveled back roads you should carry basic emergency equipment such as a shovel, chains, water, a spare tire, a jack, blankets, and some extra food and clothing. Make sure that your vehicle is in good operating condition with a full tank of gas.

Theft and vandalism occur often at trailheads. The local police can tell you of any recent problems. Try not to leave valuables in your car at all; if you must, lock them out of sight in the trunk. If I have enough room, I usually put everything in the trunk to give the car an overall empty appearance. In my many years of parking and hiking at remote trailheads, my vehicle has never been disturbed, but many of my friends' vehicles have, so be cautious.

The Hike

All of the hikes selected for this guide can be done easily by people in good physical condition. A little scrambling may be necessary for a few of the hikes, but none requires any rock-climbing skills. A few of the hikes, as noted in their descriptions, travel across vast terrain or on very faint trails. You should have an experienced hiker, along with a compass, USGS quad, and a GPS unit, with your group before attempting those hikes.

The trails are often marked with lots of exposed roots, rock cairns, or trail blazes. Most of the time the paths are very obvious and easy to follow, but the marks help when the trails are little-used and faint. Cairns are piles of rock built along the route. Tree blazes are I-shaped carvings on trees, usually at shoulder or head height. Blazes can be especially useful when a forest trail is obscured by dense vegetation. Be sure not to add your own blazes or cairns—they can confuse the route. Leave such markings to the official trail workers. Sometimes, small plastic or aluminum markers are nailed to trees to mark the route.

After reading the descriptions, pick the hike that most appeals to you. Go only as far as ability and desire allow. There is no obligation to complete any hike. Remember, you are out hiking to enjoy yourself, not to prove anything.

Miles and Directions

To help you stay on course, a detailed route finder sets forth mileages between significant landmarks along the trail.

Maps

The maps in this guide are as accurate and current as possible. When used in conjunction with the hike description, you should have little trouble following the route. I used Gaia GPS to keep me on trail and create a track of the trail while writing this book. Gaia, and other similar apps, are generally more current than the USGS topographic maps.

Most of the National Park Service areas have maps or brochures showing the trails. Excellent *National Geographic Trails Illustrated* maps are available for Haleakalā and Volcanoes National Parks. Wilderness, forest, and *Trails Illustrated* maps are usually available at park visitor centers, at Uloha–Hawai‘i's Hiking Store, and at many other outdoors shops near the trailheads. Currently most cost $10 to $15 each.

USGS topographic quadrangles are generally the most detailed and accurate maps available of natural features. With some practice they allow you to visualize peaks, canyons, cliffs, rivers, roads, and many other features. With a little experience, a topographic map, and a compass, you should never become lost. USGS quads are particularly useful for minimally used trails and off-trail travel. Unfortunately, many of the quadrangles, particularly for less-populated parts of the state, are out of date and do not show many newer man-made features such as roads and trails. However, they are still useful for their topographic information.

Most of the more developed hikes in this guide do not require a topo map. The park and forest maps and *Trails Illustrated* maps that are usually available at park headquarters and at many outdoor shops like Uloha will suffice on those trails.

GPS (Global Positioning System) units and apps, particularly those with installed maps, can be very useful for route finding when used in conjunction with paper maps. However, anyone that enters the backcountry should have at least basic knowledge in using a paper map and compass. Batteries die, and GPS units get dropped. It's best not to be completely dependent on them in case of failure. A GPS unit with maps installed can be particularly helpful on off-trail hikes.

USGS quads can usually be purchased at outdoor shops or ordered directly from USGS at http://store.usgs.gov or from online companies such as www.mytopo.com or www.topozone.com. To order from USGS, know the state, the number desired of each map, the exact map name as listed in the hike heading, and the scale.

Map Legend

Municipal

≡(H3)≡	Freeway/Interstate Highway
⊂000⊃	US Highway
⊂61⊃	State Road
⊂000⊃	County/Paved/Improved Road
= = = =	Unpaved Road
├──┼──┤	Railroad
────	Leader Line

Trails

------	Featured Trail
- - - -	Trail or Fire Road

Water Features

⬭	Body of Water
	Marsh/Swamp
	River/Creek
	Intermittent Stream
σ	Spring
≋	Waterfall

Land Management

▣	National Park/Forest
▢	State/County Park

Symbols

▰	Bench
≍	Bridge
■	Building/Point of Interest
▲	Campground
†	Cave
∧	Cemetery
→	Hike Arrow
◇	Mileage Marker
▲	Mountain/Peak
🅿	Parking
⛻	Picnic Area
🛖	Ranger Station/Park Office
🚻	Restroom
📷	Scenic View/Overlook
→	To Text
○	Towns and Cities
㉑	Trailhead
❓	Visitor/Information Center
🚰	Water

Hawai'i ("Big Island") Waterfalls

As the largest of all of the Hawaiian islands, Hawai'i Island could fit all of the other seven major islands of Hawai'i within its shores. And lucky for us, it is full of waterfalls. From the slopes of the tallest two mountains in Hawai'i, Mauna Kea and Mauna Loa, streams and rivers form and flow down to the eastern/windward coast. Trade winds bring rain clouds to the north of the island, where they water the huge grassy fields of one of America's largest cattle ranches, Parker Ranch. Rains fall even harder and whittle out deep canyons in the Kohala Mountains, forming Waipi'o and Waimanu Valleys.

Just a bit farther south the rains relentlessly pound the Hamakua Coast, creating numerous streams and making for a beautiful waterfall drive up from Hilo along Hawai'i Belt Road. If you want to see waterfalls without having to hike, this is a fantastic way to do it. Just look *mauka* (toward the mountains) as you approach each bridge and you will see many heavy-flowing falls, especially in the rainy winter season.

The rains falling high on Mauna Kea and Mauna Loa merge to create the Wailuku River, where you will find Pe'epe'e Falls, Boiling Pots, Rainbow Falls, and many others. Overwhelming at times, there is so much water flowing on the Big Island that Hilo town regularly floods! No trip to the island of Hawai'i would be complete without chasing some of its waterfalls.

1 Waianuenue ("Rainbow") Falls

Just a mile inland from the heart of Hilo, you can walk less than 100 feet of flat, well marked and maintained trail to an 80-foot-tall, very wide and strong waterfall cascading into a large pool.

Height of falls: 80 feet
Type of falls: Wide, heavily flowing plunge waterfall
Start: Wailuku River State Park, Rainbow Falls Section
Distance: 200 feet out and back
Difficulty: Easy
Hiking time: About 10 minutes (depending on how long you stay at the viewing deck)
Elevation change: 5 feet
Trail surface: Concrete path
Wheelchair accessible: Yes

Seasons/schedule: Accessible year-round. The park is open from 7:30 a.m. to 6 p.m. daily, except Hawai'i state holidays.
Fees and permits: None
Drone usage: No drones or UAS allowed
Land status: Public state park
Nearest town: Hilo
Other trail users: None
Canine compatibility: Service dogs only
Water availability: Facilities at the trailhead/parking lot

Finding the trailhead: Take Waianuenue Drive 1.7 miles up from Hilo. Turn right at the split to get on Rainbow Drive, and the parking lot will be on your right in 0.2 mile. Park in the large parking lot for the Wailuku River State Park, Rainbow Falls Section. Trailhead GPS: N19° 43.106', W155° 06.429'; Falls GPS: N19° 43.155', W155° 06.492'

The Hike

Hike from your car along the paved path to a raised observation point, and look upstream to admire the falls plunging 80 feet to a huge pool. Check out the massive cave behind the falls that has been eroded away over the years by the spray and strong currents of the falls during flash floods. The cave and the waterfall's glorious spray are indicative of the sheer power the falls creates from the constantly flowing Wailuku River. Even at a distance you can hear the waterfall's roar and feel its spray.

The Wailuku River is the second-longest river in Hawai'i, traveling about 18 miles down from where the slopes of Mauna Kea and Mauna Loa meet to the ocean near downtown Hilo. There's no way to guess what the weather is like up on top, and 18 miles is a long distance. So stay vigilant and be prepared to get away from the river if you need to.

Wailuku translates to "waters of destruction." Flash floods can occur at any time here, even on sunny days. Most days it is raining, regularly creating a rainbow across the base of the falls that lights up the dark canyon with every bright color in the color wheel.

Top: Sign at roadside
Bottom: Lookout sign

Waianuenue ("Rainbow") Falls

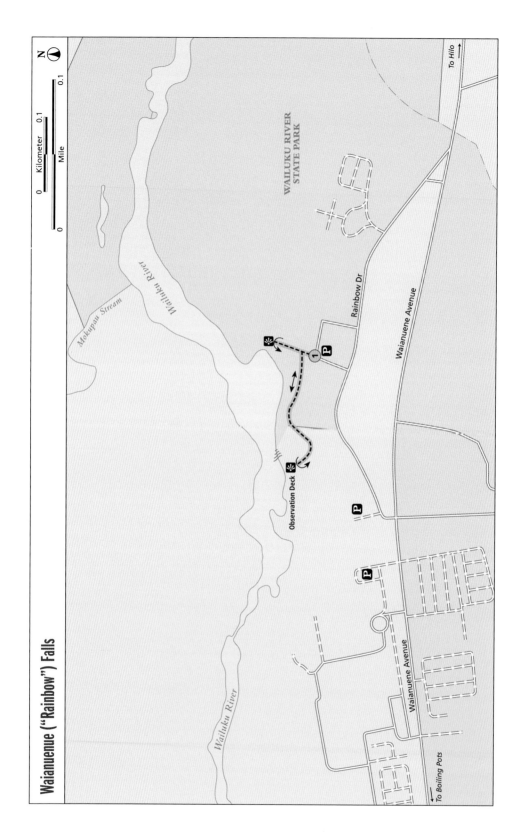

Zoomed-in view of falls

Although the hike is short, the waterfall and pool are huge. Take some time to read the various interpretive signs telling of the rich history of this magical place. For example: *Waianuenue* is translated as "rainbow water," which explains where the two names of these falls come from. On partially sunny days a rainbow can be seen in the falls. Hilo is a very wet town, with few sunny days, so if you see the sun in Hilo, especially in the morning or evening hours, make sure to go look for a rainbow being cast by Rainbow Falls.

Caution: Do not attempt to hike to the base or top of Rainbow Falls. Many have fallen off (or jumped off) to their unfortunate demise. Make sure to stay within the barriers that have been placed there for your protection.

Miles and Directions

0.0 Start at the Wailuku River State Park, Rainbow Falls Section, trailhead.

0.05 Reach a risen observation deck overlooking the Wailuku River and Rainbow Falls.

0.10 Arrive back at the trailhead.

2 Pe'epe'e Falls and Boiling Pots

From downtown Hilo, you can drive a short 3.3 miles up Waianuenue Avenue to a flat, very well marked and maintained trail overlooking a large waterfall and many small waterfalls cascading into large, turbulent pools.

Height of falls: 55 feet
Type of falls: Free-falling plunge waterfall flowing into a series of small fan falls, each with its own small pool
Start: Wailuku River State Park, Boiling Pots Section
Distance: 0.3 mile out and back
Difficulty: Easy
Hiking time: 10 to 20 minutes (depending on how long you stay at the viewing deck)
Elevation change: 5 feet
Trail surface: Concrete path

Wheelchair accessible: Yes
Seasons/schedule: Accessible year-round. The park is open from 7:30 a.m. to 6 p.m. daily, except Hawai'i state holidays.
Fees and permits: None
Drone usage: No drones or UAS allowed
Land status: Public state park
Nearest town: Hilo
Other trail users: Picnickers
Canine compatibility: Service dogs only
Water availability: Facilities at the trail entrance

Finding the trailhead: Drive 3 miles up from Hilo on Waianuenue Avenue and turn right on Pe'epe'e Falls Road. Park in the large parking lot on the right with the Wailuku River State Park, Boiling Pots Section, sign. Trailhead GPS: N19° 42.839', W155° 07.781'; Pe'epe'e Falls GPS: N19° 42.908', W155° 07.946'; Boiling Pots GPS: N19° 42.905', W155° 07.765'

The Hike

Hike from your car approximately 750 feet along the paved path to a concrete observation point. Look upstream to Pe'epe'e Falls (pronounced "pay-ay pay-ay") plunging 80 feet to a huge pool before cascading across a series of at least six other fan waterfalls, the Boiling Pots. Although these falls and pools may look inviting, please make sure to stay behind the barriers. Bring a picnic lunch, as there are picnic tables and a nice grassy lawn to spread out on.

Pe'epe'e translates to "hiding," and when you look from the observation point you will notice that much of the falls is hidden behind a rock outcropping in the middle of the stream. So look closely upstream and catch a glimpse of Pe'epe'e Falls plunging 80 feet into a huge pool.

Pe'epe'e Falls widens and narrows with the flow of the stream. One day there may only be a couple of narrow flows falling from the top, making more of a horsetail falls. Other times it can be a wide deluge of water flowing all the way across the entire width of the falls, forming more of a fan or even block type of falls. With the water of the Wailuku River coming from so high above, you could be here on a sunny day

Top: Roadside signage
Bottom: Important information about the park

Top: Pe'epe'e Falls hides behind the rock outcropping in the middle of the stream.
Bottom: A panoramic view from Pe'epe'e downstream to Boiling Pots

Pe'epe'e Falls and Boiling Pots

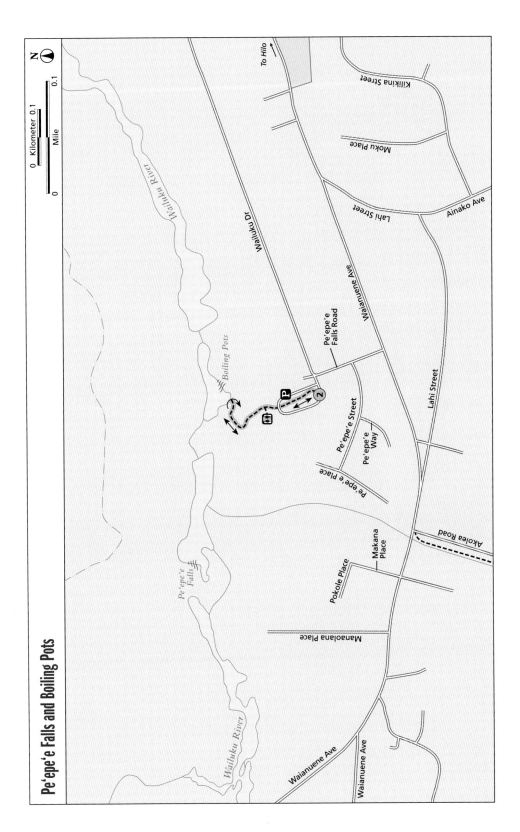

The churning pools of Boiling Pots

with a clear stream one minute, but the rains falling hard high above could change it into a raging torrent of water the next minute. It truly can happen that fast!

Below Pe'epe'e Falls are many smaller falls. These lower six waterfalls, the Boiling Pots, cascade into pot-shaped pools that appear to be boiling when the Wailuku River gets to really pumping a heavy flow. It bubbles with an energy and electricity you can feel. The water flows strong, carving large pools out of the squared-off basalt lining the streambed. These square columns were formed as the basalt lava slowly cooled, leaving us a series of really deep pools that can turn chocolate brown in flash floods or be crystal clear on calm days.

The Wailuku River is the second-longest river in Hawai'i, traveling about 18 miles down from where the slopes of Mauna Kea and Mauna Loa meet. These pools get very treacherous, pinning bathers down under the rocks along the stream banks or even washing them out into the ocean. *Do not swim here!* Many of those who have tried to swim have drowned. As inviting as it looks, just don't do it. There are plenty of great waterfalls and beaches that are much more likely to let you back out once you get in them. Mind the signs, speak with lifeguards, and talk with the locals to find many better places to swim.

Miles and Directions

0.0   Start at the Wailuku River State Park, Boiling Pots Section, trailhead.

0.15   Reach the Wailuku River overlook. Look upstream to Pe'epe'e Falls and down into the Boiling Pots.

0.3   Arrive back at the trailhead.

3 & 4 Akaka Falls and Kahuna Falls

One paved loop pathway takes you to viewpoints of two stunning waterfalls. You will encounter massive bamboo, ginger, banyan trees, and banana trees along your path through a tropical rainforest with many small falls and streams.

Height of falls: Akaka, 422 feet; Kahuna, 100 feet

Type of falls: Two heavily flowing plunge waterfalls

Start: Akaka Falls State Park main parking lot

Distance: 0.66-mile loop

Difficulty: Easy

Hiking time: About 30 minutes (depending on how long you stay at the various observation points)

Elevation change: 20 feet

Trail surface: Narrow concrete path with handrails

Wheelchair accessible: Yes

Seasons/schedule: Accessible year-round. The park is open from 8:30 a.m. to 6 p.m. daily, except Hawai'i state holidays.

Fees and permits: Parking fee (pay at the meter)

Drone usage: No drones or UAS allowed

Land status: Public state park

Nearest town: Hilo

Other trail users: None

Canine compatibility: Service dogs only

Water availability: Facilities at the trail entrance

Finding the trailhead: Take Hawai'i Belt Road HI 19 / Kamehameha Avenue 10.9 miles from Hilo. Turn left and stay on Honomu Road for 0.4 mile, then turn left on HI 220 for 0.2 mile. Turn right to stay on HI 220 for 3.3 miles and follow it to the end. Park at the large parking lot inside Akaka Falls State Park or just outside the gate. Make sure to park entirely off the pavement if you decide to park outside the gate so that others can enter and exit as necessary. Trailhead GPS: N19° 51.224', W155° 09.056'; Kahuna Falls GPS: N19° 51.402', W155° 09.070'; Akaka Falls GPS: N19° 51.179', W155° 09.283'

The Hike

The paved hike is one-way, directing you to the right (counterclockwise) at the trailhead to keep the flow of people from getting too congested at the observation points and to make the narrow pathway more enjoyable for all visitors. Start down the stairs and turn to the right. Look for the massive banyan tree 0.2 mile in on your left. You will also see lots of massive yellow bamboo in this section of the hike.

Don't miss Kahuna Falls! After passing the banyan tree on your left, make sure to look for a small turnout to your right at 0.25 mile in. Take this short side excursion to your right before heading up the trail to your left so you will not miss the Kahuna Falls viewpoint. Kahuna Falls cascades into a lush valley and falls 100 feet to the valley floor.

Continue back up the trail counterclockwise toward Akaka Falls, where you will come even closer to the massive banyan tree at 0.33 mile into your hike. Then look

Akaka Falls

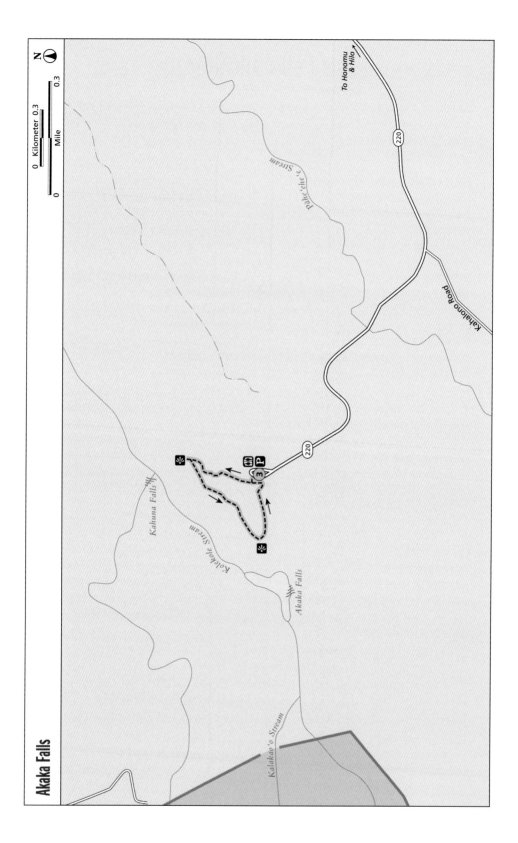

N

0 Kilometer 0.3

0 Mile 0.3

To Honomu
& Hilo

220

Kahaldno Road

Pāhe‘ehe‘e Stream

220

Kolekole Stream

Kahuna Falls

Akaka Falls

Kaliakao‘o Stream

Akaka Falls

Kahuna Falls

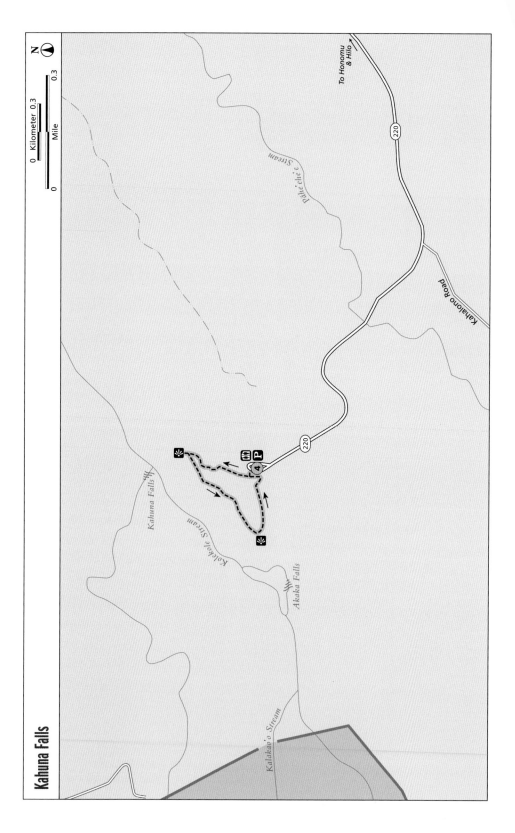

Kahuna Falls

Top: Easy stroll to Akaka Falls
Bottom: Parking lot for Akaka and Kahuna Falls hikes

for giant ginger plants on your left before descending a series of stairs to the Akaka Falls overlook. The overlook has a wide viewing area and covered benches.

Akaka Falls is 0.5 mile into your hike. Fed by the rains high above on Mauna Kea, Hawai'i's tallest mountain at 13,802 feet, Kolekole Stream has cut a deep, narrow gorge where the water free-falls down across a cliff edge and 442 feet into a large

Huge banyan tree along the trail near Kahuna Falls lookout

plunge pool below, forming Akaka Falls. Fun fact: Akaka Falls is twice the height of Niagara Falls!

Look for baby bananas growing on the banana trees at 0.55 mile into your hike, just before another small cascading falls on your right. Native birds and ferns can be witnessed throughout the lush, tropical rainforest. Remember to leave no trace so this ecosystem can continue to thrive.

Another set of two cascading falls can be found as you cross a bridge at 0.6 mile into the hike before you arrive back at the beginning of the loop. The round-trip distance is 0.66 mile, and you are now back at the main parking lot.

Important Akaka Falls State Park rules

Miles and Directions

0.0 Start at the Akaka Falls State Park trailhead.

0.25 Reach the Kahuna Falls overlook.

0.5 Reach the Akaka Falls overlook.

0.66 Arrive back at the trailhead.

5 Onomea Falls

Down a paved road off Old Mamalahoa Highway you will find the Hawaiʻi Tropical Bioreserve & Garden with lots of trails through beautiful flowers and a nice small falls with a pool just above the beautiful Onomea Bay.

Height of falls: 20 feet

Type of falls: Short but wide segment waterfall

Start: Hawaiʻi Tropical Bioreserve & Garden

Distance: 0.4 mile out and back

Difficulty: Easy

Hiking time: 30 minutes to a few hours (depending on how long you explore the gardens and bay area)

Elevation change: 92 feet from parking to the ocean

Trail surface: Concrete path

Seasons/schedule: Accessible year-round. The park is open from 9 a.m. to 5 p.m. daily, but stops selling tickets at 4 p.m. and is closed on Hawaiʻi state holidays. It is suggested that you log onto www.htbg.com or call (808) 964-5233 to reserve tickets.

Fees and permits: Fee to enter the botanical garden (free for children under 6)

Land status: Private land within the botanical garden and public land along the Onomea Bay Trail

Nearest town: Hilo

Other trail users: Botanical garden patrons and coastal hikers

Canine compatibility: Service dogs only

Water availability: Facilities at the trail entrance and throughout the botanical garden

Finding the trailhead: About 4.7 miles north of Hilo on Hawaiʻi Belt Road HI 19 / Kamehameha Avenue, turn right at the large blue highway sign that says "Scenic Route" onto Sugar Mill Road on the right side. About 1.5 miles down on the left is the Hawaiʻi Tropical Bioreserve & Garden visitor center and parking lot. Park at the large parking lot inside the botanical garden or on Old Mamalahoa Highway at one of the two Onomea Bay trailheads if you prefer to bypass the gardens. Make sure to park entirely off the pavement if you decide to park outside the gate so that others can enter and exit as necessary. Trailhead GPS: N19° 48.347', W155° 05.450'; Falls GPS: N19° 48.599', W155° 05.616'

The Hike

The main trail follows a boardwalk through the Hawaiʻi Tropical Bioreserve & Garden down toward Onomea Bay. Turn left at the Torch Ginger Trail and then the Heliconia Trail. The falls are on your right after the Palm Jungle.

The day I visited the gardens were closed, but the main corridor was still open and the falls were accessible. I started from the south entrance of the Onomea Bay Trail off the Old Mamalahoa Highway, parking and then taking in the views of the small islets and peninsulas in Onomea Bay as I hiked through the wide variety of exotic plants along the paved walkway. I then turned up Onomea Stream and the Heliconia Trail just above the Palm Jungle to find Onomea Falls.

The Onomea Bay Trail is a Nā Ala Hele trail, so it is public. If you start by going down the Onomea Bay Trail on the north side of Onomea Stream, it is an even shorter hike of 0.2 mile each way and descends approximately 200 feet from the road to the ocean. So, if you choose not to pay for access to the botanical garden, you can still view the falls, but you won't have access to the gardens. Within the gardens you will see a variety of plants (they boast to have over 2,000 species), animals such as night herons, and even another waterfall: Boulder Creek Falls.

Follow the raised wooden walkways and concrete paths throughout the 20-acre garden and down to the bay. Watch the waves pound against

Trailhead sign

View of islets in Onomea Bay

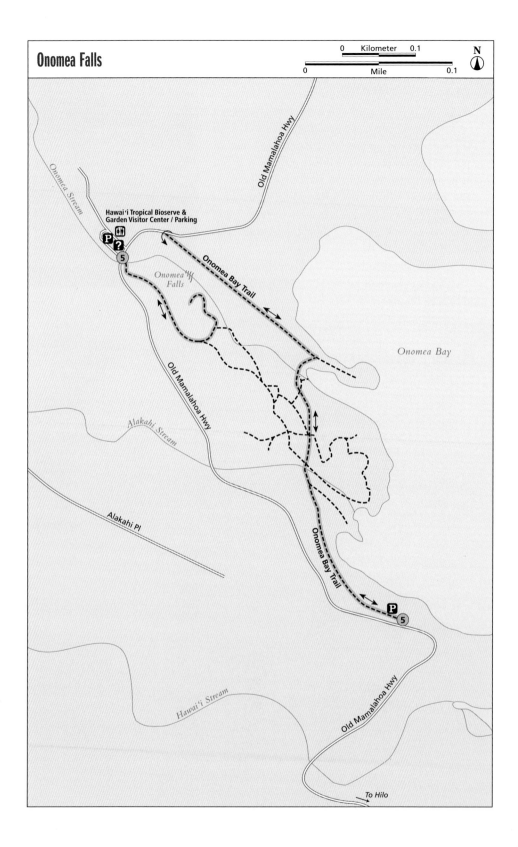

Onomea Falls

0 | Kilometer | 0.1
0 | Mile | 0.1

N

Old Mamalahoa Hwy

Onomea Stream

Hawai'i Tropical Bioserve &
Garden Visitor Center / Parking

P

5

Onomea
Falls

Onomea Bay Trail

Onomea Bay

Old Mamalahoa Hwy

Alakahi Stream

Alakahi Pl

Onomea Bay Trail

P

5

Hawai'i Stream

Old Mamalahoa Hwy

To Hilo

Stream crossing before going up to the falls

rock outcroppings, small islets, and a lush green peninsula. See Onomea Stream flowing directly into the bay, with the waves traveling up into the stream, making brackish but somehow clear water from the mixing of salty seawater and fresh stream water. And learn about how plant lovers like the botanical garden's founder, Dan Luktenhouse Sr., have worked hard to preserve these beautiful spaces for many generations to come.

Miles and Directions

From Outside the Hawai'i Tropical Bioreserve & Garden

0.0 Start at the Onomea Bay trailhead just north of the Hawai'i Tropical Bioreserve & Garden.

0.2 Proceed downhill until the trail ends at the ocean. Enjoy the views before retracing your steps.

0.4 Hike uphill on the Onomea Bay trail and watch for Onomea Falls on your left.

From Inside the Hawai'i Tropical Bioreserve & Garden

0.0 Walk to the end of the boardwalk.

0.1 Turn left at the Torch Ginger Trail and left again at the Heliconia Trail. The falls are on your right after the Palm Jungle.

0.2 Arrive back at the entrance to Hawai'i Tropical Bioreserve & Garden

Onomea Bay Trail map sign

6 Hi'ilawe Falls

A walk down a steep road into one of the most awe-inspiring valleys in Hawai'i provides views of some of the most stunning waterfalls in all of the islands. Hi'ilawe Falls at 1,450 feet tall makes a bold statement in this land of giants.

Height of falls: 1,450-foot double-tier falls with the taller tier measuring approximately 1,200 feet tall
Type of falls: Heavily flowing horsetail waterfall
Start: Waipi'o Valley Resource Center
Distance: 3.75 miles out and back to valley floor or 7.5 miles out and back to top of Muliwai Trail / Z-Trail
Difficulty: Moderate
Hiking time: 1.5 to 5 hours depending on which observation point you hike to
Elevation change: 1,200 to 2,400 feet depending on whether you climb the far side of the valley
Trail surface: Narrow concrete path with handrails to picnic area, then a steep paved road to the valley floor

Seasons/schedule: Accessible year-round. The Waipi'o Valley Resource Center is open daily, except Hawai'i state holidays.
Fees and permits: None
Land status: Private homes and land within the valley and state roads within the Kohala Forest Reserve
Nearest town: Waimea
Other trail users: Residents, hunters, and backpackers heading to Waimanu Valley
Canine compatibility: Yes, but must be kept on a leash
Water availability: Facilities at the trail entrance

Finding the trailhead: Follow Hawai'i Belt Road HI 19 / Kamehameha Avenue 39.3 miles north out of Hilo and turn right onto HI 240. Go 3.7 miles and turn left onto Mauka Cane Haul Road just past the Waipi'o Wayside Bed and Breakfast. Park at the small parking lot at the end of the road or along the sides of the road (make sure to pull completely off the pavement). If you have a four-wheel-drive vehicle (not just an all-wheel-drive vehicle), you may choose to even drive to the bottom of Waipi'o Valley. Trailhead GPS: N20° 07.039', W155° 34.932'; Falls GPS: N20° 05.901', W155° 35.632'

The Hike

Lots of local residents live both at the top of the cliff and on the valley floor. Make sure to respect them by keeping your voice down, not slamming your doors, and definitely *not trespassing* on their land.

Waipi'o Valley is about 1 mile wide and 6 miles deep. The back of the valley splits, with each towering canyon holding a massive waterfall chute at the back of it. Some, like Hi'ilawe Falls, almost always flow.

Walking down a four-wheel-drive road at the end of HI 240, you will find the Waipi'o Valley Resource Center and beginning of the Waipi'o/Waimanu Trail. Just

View from parking lot

making it to the trailhead provides a jaw-dropping view of thousand-foot cliffs, massive waterfalls flowing down them into a swamp and stream, and a huge black sand beach that hikers must traverse if they plan to go the long 10 miles to Waimanu Valley. Those hiking to Waimanu must check in at the Waipiʻo Valley Resource Center, but even those going to the bottom of the road and Waipiʻo Valley should also check in so they know to look for you if you don't make it back before dark.

There is a covered pavilion to enjoy a lunch and restrooms at the trailhead. The paved road is very steep, requiring you to put your vehicle into a low gear. Once you reach the bottom of the valley, the road is very rutted out in spots by the heavy rains that frequently occur here. The road has even been known to be completely closed at times due to the heavy downpours.

If you have a four-wheel-drive vehicle (not just all-wheel drive), you can even drive the road to the bottom of the valley. If you don't have four-wheel drive, you may still get lucky and be able to ride with someone heading down the road, or even better when heading back up. If you choose to hike it, it is approximately a 30-minute hike down to the valley floor and a little longer to get back up. Start early and keep

View into valley to see Hi'ilawe Falls. EMMA YUEN

track of how long it takes you to get down, then expect it will take you an additional 15 minutes to hike the road back up.

At the base of the hill, the road splits. Make a right turn to take you to the beach and eventually the Muliwai trail to Waimano Valley or a left turn to go up into Waipiʻo Valley and toward Hiʻilawe. If you go left and hike the road just 10 to 15 minutes into Waipiʻo Valley, you will be able to see into a narrow steep-walled canyon to Hiʻilawe Falls in the back. Feel free to view the falls from the road, but *do not* attempt to reach the base of the falls, as it is completely surrounded by private property and people's homes.

If you go across the large beach to the switchbacks going up the far side of Waipiʻo Valley, you can hike up the Muliwai Trail's many switchbacks (which is why it is also called the Z-Trail) for an hour or two to see an even better view of Hiʻilawe Falls and other waterfalls flowing into the ocean. You do not have to go to the top of the switchbacks to enjoy the various viewpoints back to Hiʻilawe. The total mileage for hiking to the top of the Muliwai Trail is approximately 7.5 miles round-trip and it is strenuous climbing the 1,200-foot walls on each side of Waipiʻo Valley.

View into Waipiʻo Valley

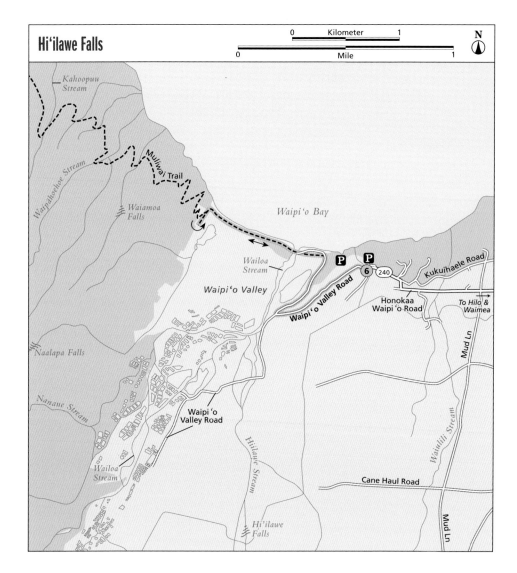

Hi'ilawe Falls

Miles and Directions

0.0 Start at the Waipi'o Valley Resource Center.

1.5 Hike to Waipi'o Valley floor. See a great view of Hi'ilawe Falls in the back of the valley, then head back up to the trailhead to finish in 3 miles. Or, continue hiking to a higher viewpoint on the Muliwai Trail.

3.75 Reach the top of the Muliwai Trail. Enjoy the views before retracing your steps.

7.5 Arrive back at the trailhead.

Kauaʻi Waterfalls

Kauaʻi may be called the "Garden Isle," but it is also full of waterfalls. As home to one of the wettest spots on Earth, Mount Waiʻaleʻale, you can imagine just how many waterfalls can form here. *Waiʻaleʻale* means "overflowing water," and the mountain receives over 400 inches of rain every year! It seems as though there is almost no dry/leeward part of Kauaʻi, as many inches of rain fall over all of the rest of the island too.

Kauaʻi is the oldest of the main Hawaiian islands, meaning its lava fields have long ago turned to rich soil that supports a lot of life. Even the dry, red dirt of Waimea Canyon is home to massive waterfalls like the 800-foot-tall Waipoʻo Falls and the Red Dirt Waterfall that seems to flow right out of the arid landscape.

Along the west side of Kauaʻi is the Nāpali Coast, with countless waterfall chutes and the constantly flowing and massive Hanakoa Falls and Hanakapiai Falls. To the north are the autumn mists of the land called Hanalei, where you can sit down, enjoy a cup of coffee or a lunch, and count numerous waterfalls in the mountains above town.

On the east side there is the Wailua River, Hawaiʻi's only navigable river, with the Fern Grotto and Uluwehi Falls (Secret Falls) hiding a few miles up it. To the south you find some arid land around Poipu Beach, but even then there is Manawaiopuna Falls (Jurassic Park Falls) and the waters flowing through Waimea Canyon hiding in the mountains just a little above it. No trip to the Garden Isle is complete without a hike to some of its waterfalls.

7 Hanakoa Falls

Take the Kalalau Trail 6 miles along the Nāpali Coast to Hanakoa Stream. Turn *mauka* (toward the mountains) and walk 0.4 more mile on a rugged, poorly marked and unmaintained trail to a 1,000-foot-tall, strong waterfall free-falling into a very large pool.

Height of falls: 1,000-foot multitier falls with the final tier measuring approximately 400 feet tall

Type of falls: Tiered plunge waterfall

Start: Kalalau Trail / Nāpali Coast trailhead

Distance: 13 miles out and back

Difficulty: Difficult

Hiking time: 8 to 10 hours (depending on how long you swim and how fast you hike the arduous Kalalau Trail). Expect to travel at a rate of approximately 2 miles per hour along the Kalalau Trail since there is so much elevation change.

Elevation change: 1,850 feet

Trail surface: Slick rocks, roots, dirt, and mud

Seasons/schedule: Accessible year-round. The park is open from 7 a.m. to 6:40 p.m. daily.

Fees and permits: Obtain the *required* permits for Nāpali Coast State Wilderness Park at www .gohaena.com. Camping permits must be acquired from Hawai'i State Parks prior to purchasing overnight parking at https://camping .ehawaii.gov. See "Additional Information."

Drone usage: No drones or UAS allowed

Land status: Public state park

Nearest town: Hanalei

Other trail users: Backpackers heading to Kalalau Beach

Canine compatibility: Yes, but must be on a leash (I've even seen one lady with two pet goats and a guy with a pet pig.)

Water availability: Facilities at the trailhead/parking lot. Lots of stream crossings to purify water along the Kalalau Trail, so you will only need to carry 1 to 2 liters of water at a time so long as you bring a purification system. *Note:* Your purification system *must* be the kind that kills *Leptospira*, the bacteria that causes leptospirosis.

Finding the trailhead: Drive 10 miles on Kuhio Highway / HI 560 north out of Princeville to the end of the road. There is a guard shack and large parking lot for those with permits. Park in the large parking lot for Hā'ena State Park, or arrive by shuttle (https://kauainsshuttle.com), and walk along the wooden boardwalk past taro fields and along the wide trail through the forest to the restrooms and showers at Ke'e Beach. The trailhead is across the street from the showers and is well marked by a yellow Kalalau Trail sign on a roofed wooden structure with a trail map and informative signage. Trailhead GPS: N22° 13.216', W159° 34.874'; Falls GPS: N22° 11.179', W159° 36.831'

The Hike

Hike from your car along the boardwalk to the trailhead. Once on the Kalalau Trail, hike up about half a mile to the cleared lookout on your right. Take a minute to look back down onto Ke'e Beach and out across Hā'ena State Park. Both Hā'ena State Park and Nāpali Coast State Wilderness Park were closed from April 2018 to June

Hanakoa Falls. Cinja Strickland

2019 following severe flooding on the north shore of Kauaʻi. Lots of work was put into improving the park facilities during this time.

You will climb over ridge after ridge, descending into valley after valley, until you reach Hanakapiai Beach in approximately 2 miles. Make sure you stop to admire the jagged cliffs and turquoise waters crashing below as you continue on your journey. You will cross multiple streams and climb out of many valleys.

Continue hiking the Nāpali Coast along the Kalalau Trail to mile marker 6. There you will find a small covered pavilion and a composting toilet. Continue past mile marker 6 and across Hanakoa Stream to the rest of the Hanakoa Campground. You will see a small trailhead sign pointing you to Hanakoa Falls on your left just a few hundred feet past Hanakoa Stream as you hike up the Kalalau Trail toward Kalalau. (**Note:** Most people use this as an overnight rest spot on their way to Kalalau Beach and don't just hike to Hanakoa Falls and Stream. The Kalalau Trail is 11 miles each way and the side jaunt to Hanakoa Falls is a little less than a half mile off of that trail at mile marker 6, so you will be adding an additional mile to your 22-mile round-trip hike to Kalalau Beach if you go to Hanakoa Falls.)

Hanakoa Falls is located up this side trail out of Hanakoa Campground 0.4 mile *mauka* (toward the mountains) of this camping area. Hike up the stream along a narrow footpath. After the slippery and difficult 0.4 mile back into the valley, you arrive at the bottom of the 1,000-foot-tall Hanakoa Falls. You can bask in the fine mist spraying off of the heavy-flowing headwall before returning to the trailhead.

Caution: There are no warning signs or ropes here to show you where a safe distance from the falls may be for such things as falling rocks. Use caution when approaching the falls or swimming in the pool. If the water is brown or starts to turn brown, be sure to turn around and leave as soon as possible. Many lives have been lost to drowning or being swept out to sea along the Nāpali Coast.

Miles and Directions

0.0 Start at the Kalalau Trail / Nāpali Coast trailhead.

2.0 Reach Hanakapiai Beach. Continue across Hanakapiai Stream and along the Kalalau Trail past Hanakapiai Beach.

6.0 Arrive at Hanakoa Campground. Take the small trail heading back into the valley after crossing Hanakoa Stream.

6.5 The trail ends at Hanakoa Falls. Enjoy the falls and pool before retracing your steps.

13.0 Arrive back at the trailhead.

Additional Information

Access is only available to those who have reserved permits to stay on the Nāpali Coast at either Hanakoa Campground or Kalalau Beach. Hanakoa is a nice overnight rest spot for those conquering the difficult and dangerous 11-mile Kalalau Trail. Remember, you just have to hike 6 miles out along the rugged Kalalau Trail to

Hanakoa Falls

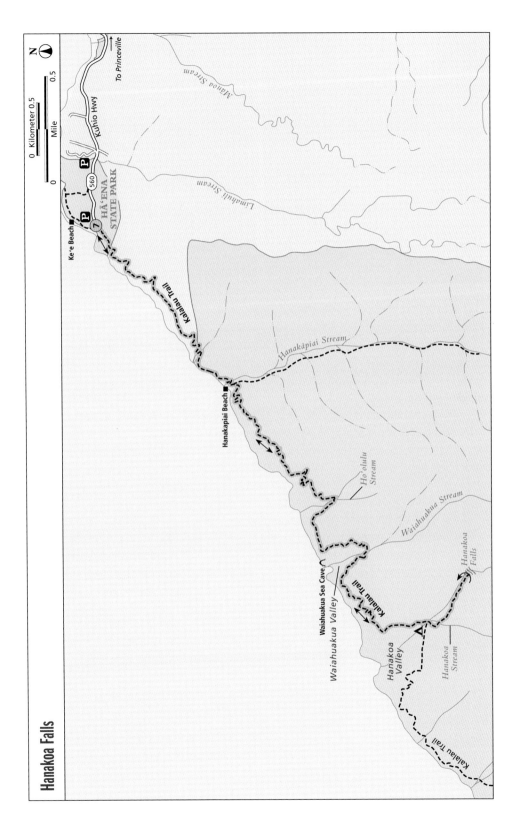

Left: Wow! What a valley. CINJA STRICKLAND
Right: Rock-hop to the big pool. CINJA STRICKLAND

Hanakoa Stream, then turn *mauka* (toward the mountains) and walk 0.4 more mile on the rugged, poorly marked and unmaintained Hanakoa Falls Trail. Many find it best to rest here after they are finished with their morning hike and afternoon swim. But oh, that cold mountain water feels so good on those achy muscles! The 1,000-foot-tall, strong waterfall free-falling into a very large pool makes it all worth it.

Permits: *Call ahead.* There is no cell reception at the trailhead / end of road, and reservations must be made at least one day before your visit. Reservations are now required (except State of Hawai'i residents★) for all vehicles, walk-in entry, and shuttle riders visiting Hā'ena State Park and can be made through the state park website: www.gohaena.com. Reservations may be made up to 30 days in advance.

Limited overnight parking is also available for campers with Kalalau overnight permits for Nāpali Coast State Wilderness Park at www.gohaena.com. Camping permits must be acquired from Hawai'i State Parks prior to purchasing overnight parking at https://camping.ehawaii.gov. Parking spots are available for purchase up to 30 days in advance, and users will be charged for the number of days their vehicle occupies the lot (e.g., a one-night stay will require paying for two days, a two-night stay will require paying for three days, etc.).

Overnight parking at Ali'i Kai Resort in Princeville is now available in coordination with the North Shore Shuttle. For more information call (808) 826-9988.

★*State of Hawai'i residents are exempt from the parking fee/reservation requirement – Proof of Hawai'i residency is required at time of entry. Proof of residency includes Hawai'i driver's license or Hawai'i state ID. Visitors to Hā'ena State Park accompanying State of Hawai'i residents are not exempt from the entry fee.*

8 Hanakapiai Falls

A 2-mile hike along the Kalalau Trail leads you to Hanakapiai Beach. Turn *mauka* (toward the mountains) from the beach and walk 2 more miles on a rugged, poorly marked and unmaintained trail to a 300-foot-tall, wide and strong waterfall free-falling into a very large pool.

Height of falls: 300 feet

Type of falls: Very strong plunge waterfall

Start: Kalalau Trail / Nāpali Coast trailhead

Distance: 8 miles out and back

Difficulty: Difficult; not for the weak hiker and very tough on the ankles

Hiking time: 6 to 8 hours (depending on how long you swim at Hanakapiai Beach and/or Hanakapiai Falls)

Elevation change: 700 feet each way

Trail surface: Slick rocks, roots, dirt, and mud

Seasons/schedule: Accessible year-round. The park is open from 7 a.m. to 6:40 p.m. daily.

Fees and permits: Obtain the *required* permits for Nāpali Coast State Wilderness Park at www .gohaena.com. Camping permits must be acquired from Hawai'i State Parks prior to pur-chasing overnight parking at https://camping .ehawaii.gov. See "Additional Information."

Drone usage: No drones or UAS allowed

Land status: Public state park

Nearest town: Hanalei

Other trail users: Backpackers to Kalalau Beach and swimmers going to Hanakapiai Beach from Ke'e Beach

Canine compatibility: Yes, but must be on a leash (I've even seen one lady with two pet goats and a guy with a pet pig.)

Water availability: Facilities at the trailhead/ parking lot. Lots of stream crossings to purify water along the Kalalau Trail, so you will only need to carry 1 to 2 liters of water at a time so long as you bring a purification system. *Note:* Your purification system *must* be the kind that kills *Leptospira*, the bacteria that causes leptospirosis.

Finding the trailhead: Drive 10 miles on Kuhio Highway / HI 560 north out of Princeville to the end of the road. There is a guard shack and large parking lot for those with permits. Park in the large parking lot for Hā'ena State Park, or arrive by shuttle (https://kauainsshuttle.com), and walk along the wooden boardwalk past taro fields and along the wide trail through the forest to the restrooms and showers at Ke'e Beach. The trailhead is across the street from the showers and is well marked by a yellow Kalalau Trail sign on a roofed wooden structure with a trail map and informative signage. Trailhead GPS: N22° 13.216', W159° 34.874'; Falls GPS: N22° 11.123', W159° 35.610'

The Hike

Hike from your car along the boardwalk to the trailhead. Once on the Kalalau Trail, you will climb over ridge after ridge, descending into valley after valley, until you reach Hanakapiai Beach in approximately 2 miles. Admire the jagged cliffs and tur-quoise waters crashing below along this section of your journey. Make sure to look

back north at approximately 0.5 mile and down onto Keʻe Beach and out across Hāʻena State Park. Both Hāʻena State Park and Nāpali Coast State Wilderness Park were closed from April 2018 to June 2019 following severe flooding on the north shore of Kauaʻi and a landslide that closed the road. Lots of work was put into improving the park facilities during this time.

Once you reach Hanakapiai Beach, turn inland and follow the trail straight back into the valley (to the left of the outhouse / primitive bathroom) across an ancient rock wall and into a clearing made for a helicopter to land. In the clearing you will observe a maintenance shed on your right. Continue on the rugged trail 2 more miles, crossing the stream multiple times until you reach the very back of Hanakapiai Valley and the base of Hanakapiai Falls. Swim in the huge pool of cold stream water, but remember how long the hike in took and have a turn-around time that allows you to climb the steep ridges back to the parking lot well before the park gates close at 6:40 p.m.

You will encounter lots of guava, strawberry guava, lilikoi (passion fruit), and even a couple of orange trees on your way back into the valley. The trail will cross the stream many times and will go through sections of deep mud, making it pointless to try to keep your shoes clean or dry. The spoils of a massive flowing waterfall with a giant pool to swim in go to those who embrace the wet, muddy environment. Have good traction on your shoes (preferably deep lugs like the Altra Lone Peak or Salomon Speedcross) to keep from sliding any more than necessary, and be ready to trudge through what seem to be the longest 2 miles of hiking in the world.

Some days you get to see multiple waterfalls all along the canyon walls as you make your way to the very back of the valley and to the headwall where Hanakapiai flows down from the Hono O Nā Pali Natural Area Reserve. Take breaks to take in the views of this magical place. Watch your steps as you rock-hop and your head as you duck under limbs. ***Caution:*** There are no warning signs or ropes here to show you where a safe distance from the falls and any potentially falling rocks may be. Use caution when approaching the falls or swimming in the pool. If the water is brown or starts to turn brown, be sure to turn around and leave as soon as possible. Many lives have been lost attempting to cross Hanakapiai Stream.

I once met a gentleman searching the cliff edges along the Kalalau Trail about halfway to Hanakapiai Beach. I asked him what he was looking for, and he said it was his cell phone. I asked what it looked like and started looking with him. He eventually explained that he had lost his phone somewhere in this area the night before. He and his wife had started early and hiked to Hanakapiai Falls. They were on their way back from the falls when his wife took a bad step and broke her leg! There is no cell reception there, and with the broken leg they were moving much slower on the way back.

Night fell as they were making their way out to find help. He brought out the only light he had—his cell phone. As they were walking along the treacherous trail, he

◄ *Hanakapiai Falls.* Nandor Szotak

Beautiful blue pool. NANDOR SZOTAK

slipped and dropped the phone. It fell over the side, down the cliff, and he could not get to it. They walked the rest of the way out in the dark! Now it was the next day and his wife was being cared for at the hospital in Lihue. I helped him look as long as I thought was safe for me to be able to get back in the daylight, and I wished him the best. I hope he found his cell phone and his wife healed up. I also hope they have made it back and hiked to Hanakapiai Falls again, but this time without any incident.

Miles and Directions

0.0   Start at the Kalalau Trail / Nāpali Coast trailhead.

2.0   Arrive at Hanakapiai Beach. Turn off of the Kalalau Trail to your left, walking back into Hanakapiai Valley shortly after crossing Hanakapiai Stream.

4.0   The trail ends at Hanakapiai Falls. Enjoy the falls and pool before retracing your steps.

8.0   Arrive back at the trailhead.

Additional Information

Permits: *Call ahead.* There is no cell reception at the trailhead / end of road, and reservations must be made at least one day before your visit. Reservations are now required (except State of Hawai'i residents★) for all vehicles, walk-in entry, and shuttle riders visiting Hā'ena State Park and can be made through the state park website: www.gohaena.com. Reservations may be made up to 30 days in advance.

Hanakapiai Falls

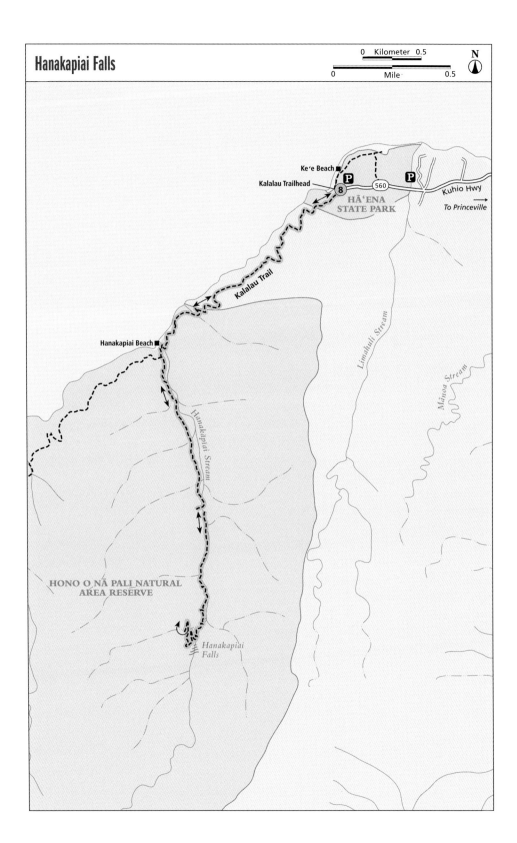

0 Kilometer 0.5

0 Mile 0.5

N

Keʻe Beach ■

Kalalau Trailhead

P

8

560

P

Kuhio Hwy

HĀʻENA
STATE PARK

To Princeville

Limahuli Stream

Mānoa Stream

Kalalau Trail

Hanakapiai Beach ■

Hanakapiai Stream

HONO O NĀ PALI NATURAL
AREA RESERVE

Hanakapiai
Falls

Left: *Big flow makes for a fun swim.*
Right: *The towering falls sound like thunder raining down.*

Limited overnight parking is also available for campers with Kalalau overnight permits for Nāpali Coast State Wilderness Park at www.gohaena.com. Camping permits must be acquired from Hawai'i State Parks prior to purchasing overnight parking at https://camping.ehawaii.gov. Parking spots are available for purchase up to 30 days in advance, and users will be charged for the number of days their vehicle occupies the lot (e.g., a one-night stay will require paying for two days, a two-night stay will require paying for three days, etc.).

Overnight parking at Ali'i Kai Resort in Princeville is now available in coordination with the North Shore Shuttle. For more information call (808) 826-9988.

⋆ *State of Hawai'i residents are exempt from the parking fee/reservation requirement. Proof of Hawai'i residency is required at time of entry. Proof of residency includes Hawai'i driver's license or Hawai'i state ID. Visitors to Hā'ena State Park accompanying State of Hawai'i residents are not exempt from the entry fee.*

9 Kilauea Falls / Stone Dam

At Anaina Hou Community Park near Kiluaea you will find putt-putt golf, a climb-ing wall, a playground, the Chocolate Factory, and Aloha Oha Farms. Hiking approxi-mately 1.75 miles from this community park leads you to a wide falls flowing over an old stone dam with a large swimming pool above it. The swimming pool has a diving platform with a ladder to climb out, and two rope swings to swing off into the cool stream water. There are even a few large fields to picnic in!

Height of falls: 25 feet
Type of falls: Wide block falls over a stone dam
Start: The primary trailhead was at Anaina Hou Community Park, with a secondary, shorter hike from the North Shore Dog Park. As of the time of this writing, however, the Anaina Hou Community Park entrance has been closed for many months, possibly due to COVID-19, so the primary trailhead now seems to be at the North Shore Dog Park.
Distance: 3.5 miles out and back
Difficulty: Easy
Hiking time: 1 to 1.5 hours (depending on how long you swim and/or picnic at the falls)
Elevation change: 100 feet

Trail surface: Mostly flat, wide-open trails through fields, but some slick rocks, roots, and mud
Seasons/schedule: Accessible year-round
Fees and permits: None
Land status: Private land (Wai Koa Plantation)
Nearest town: Kilauea
Other trail users: Fruit and vegetable farmers
Canine compatibility: Yes, but must be on a leash
Water availability: Facilities at the trailhead at Anaina Hou Community Park. No facilities at the North Shore Dog Park. Stream water at the falls, which must be purified due to the risk of leptospirosis throughout the Hawai'i islands.

Finding the trailhead: Take Kuhio Highway / HI 560 for 3.6 miles south from Princeville and turn right on Kahililholo Road. Drive 0.6 mile and turn left into the North Shore Dog Park. Park at the dog park and hike to your left past the farming gate at the end of the concrete parking lot. Trailhead GPS: N22° 12.304', W159° 25.521'; Falls GPS: N22° 11.318', W159° 25.218'

The Hike

From North Shore Dog Park

Hike from your car to the left end of the parking lot and past the farming gate with a yellow sign that says "Stone Dam Mini Golf" and brown sign that says "Unauthor-ized Vehicles Prohibited." Stay straight onto a grass road/trail. Enjoy the eucalyptus grove and wild ginger on your right. Turn right at the Stone Dam sign at approxi-mately 0.4 mile, then turn right again at 0.74 mile. Continue as it explains in "For Both Trails" below.

Buddha overlooks a large grassy field below the dam.

From Anaina Hou Community Park

Hike from your car out the bottom of the gravel parking lot and through the open gate. If the gate is closed and the trail is closed, proceed through the North Shore Dog Park. Once on the Wai Koa Loop Trail, you will go downhill, curving to a streambed. Cross the stream and climb slightly back to an open field following the trail signs. Go 0.85 mile to the intersection with the trail coming from the North Shore Dog Park. Continue as it explains in "For Both Trails" below, adding 0.1 mile to each mileage amount stated.

For Both Trails

Walk along a beautiful tree-lined and leaf-covered trail, which can get muddy in spots. Follow the trail slightly left at 0.85 mile, then take a slight right at Wishing Horse Farm at 0.9 mile. It changes to an open field and then back into another forest at 0.95 mile. You will likely see various fruits and vegetables growing in the fields along your way to the falls. *Do not pick the produce.* This is an active farm and a food source for many Hawaiians. Picking a fruit is theft.

Stay on the trail until you emerge back out of the eucalyptus trees at 1.25 miles and cross the field to the left, following the path. Look for the next trail signs at 1.33 miles and follow a gravel road to a white sign saying "May Peace Prevail on Earth" at around 1.5 miles. Stay right to go to a pavilion on a cliff with a view overlooking the fields and the falls, or go down to your left to a large grassy field full of various types of ginger plants and eventually the base of the falls.

Arrive at the dam with the waterfall flowing over it and a large pool with koi fish below it at 1.75 miles. (***Fun fact:*** This concrete dam was completed in 1880 and was

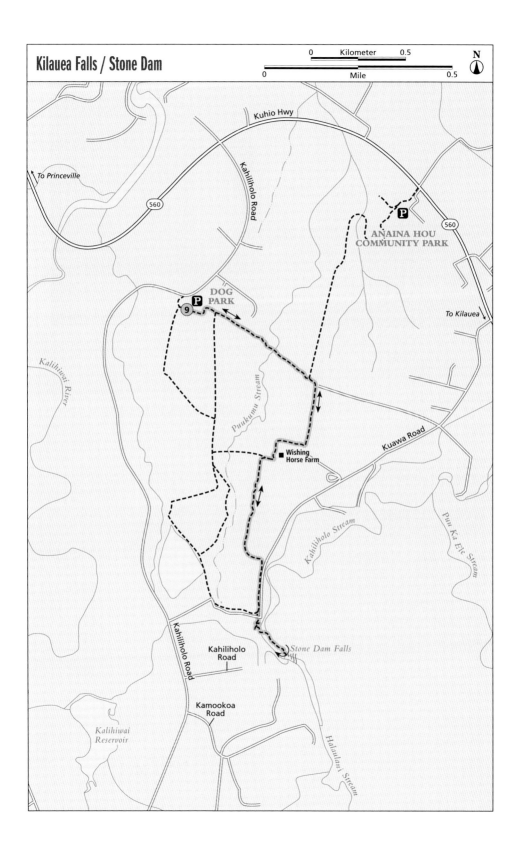

Kilauea Falls / Stone Dam

Kilometer
0   0.5

Mile
0   0.5

N

To Princeville

Kuhio Hwy

560

Kahiliholo Road

ANAINA HOU
COMMUNITY PARK

P

560

To Kilauea

DOG
PARK

P

9

Kalihiwai River

Puukumu Stream

Kuawa Road

Wishing
Horse Farm

Kahiliholo Stream

Puu Ka Ele Stream

Kahiliholo
Road

Kahiliholo
Road

Kamookoa
Road

Kalihiwai
Reservoir

Stone Dam Falls

Halaulani Stream

Stone waterfall with large pool above it

built for sugarcane irrigation.) Continue to the immediate right of the dam and up a concrete path with a handrail. Climb the stairs to the top of the dam to find a much larger pool with two rope swings, a platform to climb out and jump from, and a large mowed grass field to picnic in. There are often families and a variety of other people enjoying the fields and pool. (***Note:*** Use great caution when swimming in the pool, especially when jumping in or using the rope swings.)

Follow the trail up and loop around to the right after climbing the stairs to see native Hawaiian ferns, monster yellow bamboo, green bamboo, and a Buddha statue. This hill gives you a nice view of the gardens, pool, and fields below. Bring a book or a hammock and stay a while. You'll be glad you did.

Miles and Directions

0.0 Start at the North Shore Dog Park trailhead. Walk out of the dog park to your left and past the farming gate.

0.4 Turn right at the Stone Dam sign.

0.74 Turn right and follow the main trail.

0.9 Make a slight right at Wishing Horse Farm.

1.25 Emerge from eucalyptus forest into an open field and continue to your left on the path.

1.5 Reach a white sign that says "May Peace Prevail on Earth." Turn left to go through an open field to the base of the falls.

1.75 The trail ends at a stone dam with a waterfall pouring over it and a large pool above it. Enjoy the views before retracing your steps.

3.5 Arrive back at the trailhead.

10 Ho'opi'i Falls

Near the end of Kapahi Road above Kapa'a, you can find a trailhead leading out of a neighborhood to two sets of waterfalls and a nice cool swimming hole complete with rope swing.

Height of falls: 20 feet
Type of falls: Segment
Start: Trailhead near end of Kapahi Road
Distance: 2.14 miles out and back
Difficulty: Moderate
Hiking time: 1 to 2 hours (depending on how long you swim and enjoy the falls)
Elevation change: Approximately 50 feet
Trail surface: Slick rocks, roots, dirt, and mud
Seasons/schedule: Accessible year-round
Fees and permits: None
Land status: Private land. Be sure to respect the land and neighborhood here, as it could be closed anytime.

Nearest town: Kapa'a
Other trail users: Homeless people from time to time
Canine compatibility: Yes, but must be on a leash
Water availability: Stream water along the way and at the falls, which must be purified due to the risk of leptospirosis throughout the Hawai'i islands. Be sure to bring plenty of water and snacks but leave no trash—pack out what you pack in.

Finding the trailhead: Take Kaapuni Road 1 mile from Kapa'a. Turn right onto Kawaihau Road and make a slight left onto Kapahi Road. Watch to your left after turning off of Kawaihau Road onto Kapahi Road for a power pole marked with a yellow and black "Caution: Be Quiet" sign and yellow reflectors below it. This is the trailhead. Park in one of the dirt pull-offs just before the end of Kapahi Road. *Do not* talk loud, play loud music, or slam your doors. We want everyone to be able to enjoy this trail for generations to come. Trailhead GPS: N22° 06.175', W159° 20.507'; Falls GPS: N22° 06.309', W159° 20.243'

The Hike

Hike from your car on Kapahi Road past the tall guinea/California grass and yellow "Caution: Be Quiet" sign. Once on the trail, you will descend gradually, following a heavily traveled path. This area is most often frequented by locals, but is becoming more and more popular among all waterfall enthusiasts.

Follow the slick, heavily traveled trail on a gradual descent to the first set of falls. Pass under an overhead hau tree tangle at 0.15 mile and watch for lilikoi (passion fruit) vines and banana trees. The trail will meet up with the stream at 0.27 mile in an open forest of very large Albizia trees. These are the huge trees you might remember from the major motion picture *Jurassic Park*, the opening scene of which was filmed at Ho'opi'i Falls!

The large falls makes an even bigger pool.

Avoid the dinosaurs as you walk beside the stream. Don't cross it! Instead, keep it on your left as you head downstream toward the falls. There is a fun bouldering-type move (around a bulbous rock protruding out toward the stream) you can make at 0.35 mile to keep your feet dry, or just go ahead and hike through the water to keep from potentially sliding or falling in.

You will reach the first set of falls, the smaller falls with a few pools, at 0.45 mile into your hike. Feel free to stay a while and play in these falls until you are ready to head on down to the larger Hoʻopiʻi Falls.

Continue up the trail, past more hanging hau tree branches, to a well-defined dirt path. Take a left and walk through a grove of strawberry guava. You will come to a very large tree at 0.6 mile and an intersection at 0.65 mile. Turn left at the intersection and walk through a dreamlike grassy meadow at 0.75 mile.

Stay along the stream to arrive at a second, larger set of falls at 1.07 miles into your journey. This is Hoʻopiʻi Falls. You have made it to the top of the falls and can take in

Ho'opi'i Falls

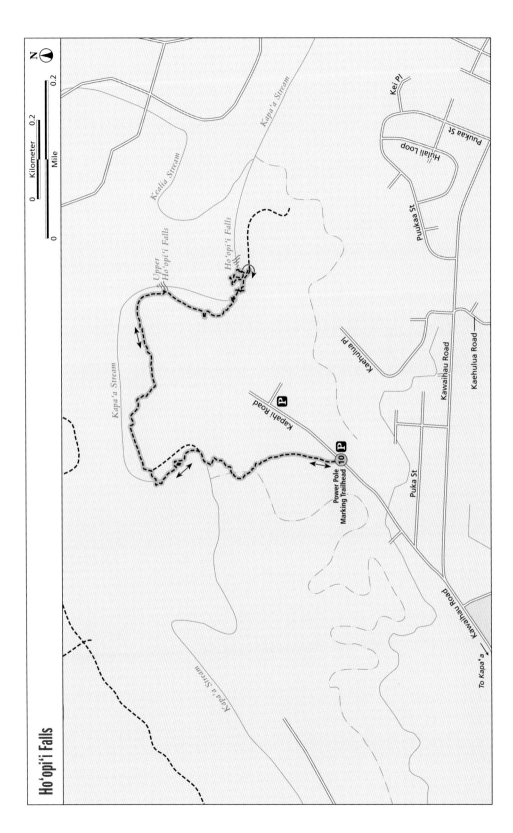

the view down its cascading waters into the very large pool below. Continue along the trail and turn down a well-worn path to your left, using various hau tree branches as handrails, to access the bottom of the falls and a swimming pool complete with a rope swing at 1.2 miles into your hike.

Note: When hiking back out, you will pass the first falls again and then you must watch for the very large tree to know when to turn uphill and stay on the main trail as you make your way back to your vehicle. The main trail will be well worn and easily identifiable as the main trail. I often call such trails an "elephant trail," as it appears as if a herd of elephants has walked through there.

Miles and Directions

0.0 Start at the trailhead on the left near the end of Kapahi Road: a power pole marked with a yellow "Caution: Be Quiet" sign and yellow reflectors below it. Go down through the guinea grass.

0.27 Meet up with the stream. Hike down the streamside trail.

0.45 Enjoy views of the first set of falls. Continue down the stream by going up the hill and turning left at the well-defined path.

0.65 Turn left at the intersection and hike down the stream.

1.07 Arrive at the second, larger Ho'opi'i Falls. Enjoy the view and the pool before retracing your steps. Make sure to stay on the well-worn trail, turning up away from the stream at the large tree above the first falls.

2.14 Arrive back at the trailhead.

11 ʻOpaekaʻa Falls

In Wailua River State Park and up Kuamoʻo Road from Kapaʻa, you find the 151-foot-tall ʻOpaekaʻa Falls. The falls often have multiple different waterfalls flowing around a tree in the center of them.

Height of falls: 151 feet
Type of falls: Wide plunge
Start: ʻOpaekaʻa Falls overlook at Wailua River State Park
Distance: 600 feet out and back
Difficulty: Easy
Hiking time: 10 to 30 minutes (depending on how many pictures you take and whether you take time to take in the sights and read the interpretive signs)
Elevation change: 0 feet
Trail surface: Paved sidewalk

Wheelchair accessible: Yes
Seasons/schedule: Accessible year-round
Fees and permits: None
Land status: Public state park
Nearest town: Wailua isn't really a town, so the nearest town actually is Kapaʻa.
Other trail users: People hiking the Wailua Heritage Trail and bird-watchers
Canine compatibility: Yes, but must be on a leash
Water availability: Facilities at the trailhead/ parking lot

Finding the trailhead: Turn onto HI 580 / Kaumoʻo Road off HI 56. Drive upland 1.9 miles and park at the large parking lot on your right at the overlook for ʻOpaekaʻa Falls at Wailua River State Park. Trailhead GPS: N22° 02.787', W159° 21.493'; Falls GPS: N22° 02.889', W159° 21.713'

The Hike

Hike from your car to the large overlook of the falls, and admire the majestic 151-foot-tall waterfall with its pumping flow of water from the Wailua River. The Wailua River is Hawaiʻi's only navigable river. It is fed from Waiʻaleʻale, one of the wettest spots on Earth! You may want to bring a picnic lunch, as there is even a picnic table at the overlook.

The name *ʻOpaekaʻa* means "rolling shrimp," *ʻopae* being Hawaiian for "shrimp" and *kaʻa* for "rolling." Hawaiʻi's native freshwater shrimp used to be plentiful in this stream. Like salmon, these mountain shrimp, *Ōpaekalaʻole*, can go upriver. Unlike salmon, they can actually climb pretty large waterfalls along their path. Many of these shrimp would climb up this 151-foot falls and eventually fall, or "roll," back down it.

Miles and Directions

0.0 Park at the roadside stop for ʻOpaekaʻa Falls at Wailua River State Park.

50 ft. Reach the ʻOpaekaʻa Falls overlook. Follow the paved trail to the various overlooks and spectacular views of the area.

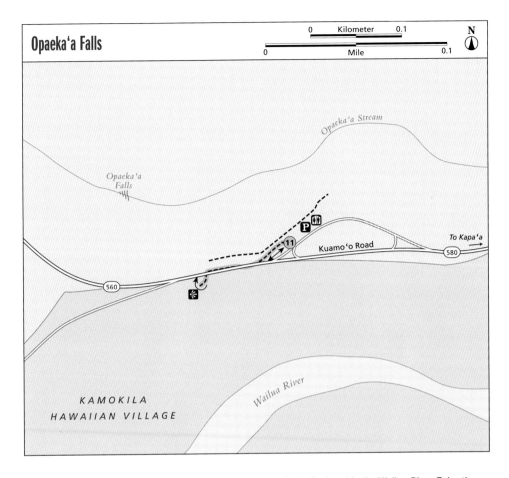

Opaeka'a Falls

0 — Kilometer — 0.1

0 — Mile — 0.1

N

Opaeka'a Stream

Opaeka'a Falls

To Kapa'a →

580

Kuamo'o Road

11

560

KAMOKILA
HAWAIIAN VILLAGE

Wailua River

300 ft. The trail crosses the road and goes to an overlook of a bend in the Wailua River. Enjoy the views before retracing your steps.

600 ft. Arrive back at the trailhead.

Additional Information

After taking in the falls from the overlook, continue toward the mountains on the Wailua Heritage Trail. Cross Kuamo'o Road to find a view of a large bend in the Wailua River. You can even see down to the restored native Hawaiian village of Kamokila, where they demonstrate and explain how the ancient Hawaiians lived off the land, preserving their culture and people for thousands of years on a diet of such things as kalo/taro, pig, coconuts, and fish. Thousands of miles from the nearest civilization, these verdant valleys sustained thousands of residents. Take in the views down

◀ *Top: A view from the parking lot into the verdant valley*
Bottom: A closer look shows how large the falls are.

Follow the trail across the road to see the Wailua River.

toward Secret Falls and the Fern Grotto. Follow the Wailua Heritage Trail to its end to see up the mountains toward Mount Waiʻaleʻale.

Take time to read the various interpretive signs informing you about the area. The first sign tells of Waiʻaleʻale, often the wettest spot on Earth, which regularly sees 400 to 600 inches of rainfall each year. This rainfall forms the large Alakai Swamp, which feeds Hanakoa, Hanakapiai, Waipoʻo, and many of the great waterfalls on Kauaʻi. Way above these falls is Kawaikini, the highest point on Kauaʻi at 5,243 feet.

Ahupuaʻas were how the islands were initially divided up, oftentimes having the region based around a source of water such as a river or stream, and they provided all of the water, food, and resources needed to sustain a community. The second interpretive sign tells of Maunakapu and the Wailua River. The mountain ridges of Maunakapu and Nounou divide the Wailua *ahupuaʻa* into two sections: Wailua Kai and Wailua Uka. Together, the two regions of this verdant valley provided all of the resources and necessities to support the people of this region. Read about how the local population here cultivated the land and provided crops for the ruling *aliʻi* (royalty).

Note: Opaekaʻa Falls is sometimes also referred to as Hoʻolalaea Waterfall.

◄ *Multiple waterfalls flow across the face.* Nandor Szotak

12 Wailua Falls

At a roadside overlook you will see the majestic 173-foot-tall Wailua Falls, which is a heavily flowing waterfall on the South Fork Wailua River near Lihue.

Height of falls: 173 feet
Type of falls: Fan
Start: Wailua Falls Overlook
Distance: 300 feet out and back
Difficulty: Easy
Hiking time: 10 to 30 minutes (depending on how many pictures you take and whether you take time to take in the sights and read the interpretive signs)
Elevation change: 0 feet

Trail surface: Pavement
Seasons/schedule: Accessible year-round
Fees and permits: None
Land status: Public state park
Nearest town: Lihue
Other trail users: None
Canine compatibility: Yes, but must be on a leash
Water availability: None

Finding the trailhead: Drive up Maalo Road (HI 583) 3.9 miles from the town of Lihue to the end of the road. Park in one of the four stalls at the Wailua Falls Overlook. If the stalls are full, you may consider parking along the road in a pull-off or coming back another day. Make sure to park your car entirely off of the road to avoid being ticketed. Look for the fenced overlook with breathtaking views of the falls. Trailhead GPS: N22° 02.029', W159° 22.648'; Falls GPS: N22° 02.069', W159° 22.629'

The Hike

Drive all the way to the end of Maalo Road / HI 583 to find a cul-de-sac with parking spots. Hike from your car to the overlook on the edge of the paved road. Make sure to watch for other cars and keep your kids and pets close to you, as this area can get very busy.

Enjoy the overlook, looking down on the falls, the huge pool, and oftentimes the visible rock beach below. If the water is brown or the rock beach is not visible, it is likely a sign of the river experiencing a flash flood! Most days the level of the flow creates two waterfalls—if there is only one large brown waterfall, then the Wailua River is in a flash flood stage. *Caution:* Heed the warning signs and stay behind the railings and fences, as many people have been injured or killed trying to access the falls due to very steep cliffs and flash floods that often occur in this very rainy region of the island.

Wailua Falls is known for creating beautiful rainbows in its mist on sunny days. The dramatic double waterfall is featured in the opening credits of the popular late 1970s and early 1980s TV show *Fantasy Island*. A truly iconic sight, you can also find it on many Hawai'i souvenirs and postcards. You won't want to miss this beauty.

Wailua Falls

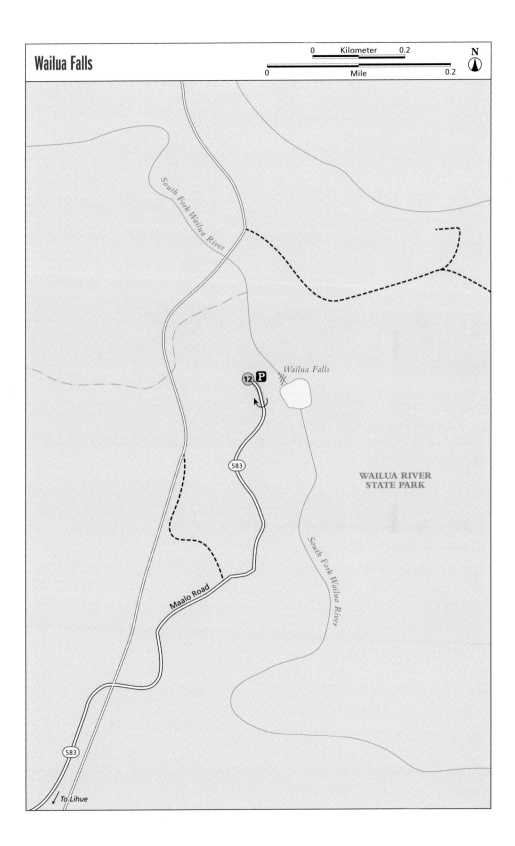

0   Kilometer   0.2

0   Mile   0.2

N

South Fork Wailua River

Wailua Falls

12 P

583

WAILUA RIVER
STATE PARK

South Fork Wailua River

Maalo Road

583

To Lihue

Wailua Falls flows heavily into a large pool. Nandor Szotak

Miles and Directions

More of a drive than a hike, walk approximately 150 feet to the overlook and take in the majestic view of the falls.

13 Uluwehi Falls (Secret Falls)

For this "hike" you will first need a vessel to carry you up Hawai'i's only navigable waterway, the Wailua River. Kayak or paddle up the river to the trailhead for a rugged, unmaintained trail to a 120-foot-tall waterfall and nice swimming pool. Rent a kayak or stand-up paddleboard and go alone, or choose an outfitter who will guide you to the falls and provide you lunch. This adventure up a river and over land awaits those who have both strong arms and strong legs!

Height of falls: 120 feet

Type of falls: Plunge

Start: North Fork Wailua River. To reach this trail, you must first secure a kayak or stand-up paddleboard. See "Additional Information."

Distance: 2.24 miles round-trip hike plus anywhere from a 0.8-mile to 4-mile paddle, depending on where you launch

Difficulty: Moderate trail, but the paddling makes it a full-body workout, especially in the afternoon when the trade winds are blowing in your face as you try to paddle down the river.

Hiking time: 2 to 6 hours (depending on how long you swim and how much adventuring you do while paddling)

Elevation change: 130 feet

Trail surface: Some boardwalk mixed with slick rocks, roots, dirt, and mud

Seasons/schedule: Accessible year-round. Most outfitters require their boats returned by 4 or 5 p.m.

Fees and permits: None for the hike, but you may have to pay for your boat to get to the trailhead.

Land status: Public state park

Nearest town: Kapa'a

Other trail users: None

Canine compatibility: Yes, but must be on a leash

Water availability: Your outfitter may provide water for free or for a fee. Otherwise, stream water that must be purified.

Finding the trailhead: Just up the Wailua River, park at the launch, or arrive by shuttle, and kayak or SUP to the trailhead. The trailhead is a large rock and sand beach area on the North Fork Wailua River. See "Additional Information." Trailhead GPS: N22° 02.617', W159° 21.702'; Falls GPS: N22° 02.957', W159° 22.274'

The Hike

Start by renting a kayak or stand-up paddleboard (SUP) from an outfitter, or borrowing one from a friend on Kaua'i. You can launch your vessel from the Wailua State Park Boat Ramp or from facilities across the river if you are going with an outfitter. Once you have paddled up the Wailua River 1.8 miles from the launch sites near Kuhio Highway / HI 56, you can look to your right to see the Kamokila Hawaiian Village, a traditional Hawaiian village re-created on the banks of the Wailua River. They say native Hawaiians have been living in this area for over 1,500 years!

At 120 feet tall, Uluwehi Falls fills the small valley. NANDOR SZOTAK

Once you have passed the Kamokila Village, continue up the Wailua River until it splits and then turn right to go toward the falls (left goes to Fern Grotto). Paddle through the more and more narrow stream until you come to a large sandy spot to beach your kayak or SUP on the right bank of the river. Your hiking adventure to Uluwehi Falls (aka Secret Falls) begins here.

Hike from the beach and along the path heading up the river, going in and out of the dense guinea grass. Stay along the stream, the North Fork of the Wailua River, until you cross over it to the left at 0.15 mile into your hike. The trail on the right side of the river will have disappeared, and you will likely see a rocky island in the middle and a small sign on the far bank of the river. Turn left and cross the river. Continue your hike up a short muddy embankment, following the heavily traveled trail through dense jungle undergrowth with lots of roots and mud. Enjoy lots of wild ginger and drooping hau trees along your path before it goes back into very thick guinea grass.

You will then come upon a boardwalk at 0.35 mile into your hike and will continue along the boardwalk until 0.52 mile. The boardwalk ends for a few feet before resuming a couple more times and finally ends for good at 0.6 mile. The trail then

◀ *Top: Stay on the boardwalk so we can all enjoy the wildflowers.*
Bottom: Cross in front of a small falls at 0.92 mile.

Hikers settle in for lunch with a view.

opens up into an Albizia and mango forest with lots of ferns and flowering ground cover before going back into a boardwalk at 0.8 mile.

Continue following the trail along the riverbank and past a cement tower with a water-level gauge at 0.82 mile. The rock-hopping will now commence—beware: they are slick! You will encounter one final section of boardwalk at 0.9 mile before two stream crossings and some small falls at 0.92 mile. Follow the trail sign that leads you to turn left, heading away from the river and climbing up a short, steep, and muddy section. This will lead you into another canyon.

At the top you will cross a small stream again (there is usually a rope to help steady you here). Listen for the native forest birds to sing to you along your final stretch of trail to Uluwehi Falls. You will reach the falls at 1.12 miles into your hike. Enjoy a dip in the pool or take in the view from a shaded spot on the riverbank. The water free-falls off the cliff over 100 feet to splash down directly into the pool.

Caution: There are no warning signs or ropes here to show you where a safe distance from the cliff edge is. Don't get too close to the cliffs, as rocks and other debris sometimes fall down. Do not attempt to cross the stream if the water has covered all of the rocks or is brown, as this is a sign that flash flooding is occurring. When in doubt, keep out. Turn around, don't drown.

Located on the Lower Wailua River on Kaua'i's east side, the river is subject to strong winds and water flow that can vary greatly, making the paddling portion of the journey difficult and even dangerous for those who aren't in good physical shape. Remember to stay on the right side of the river as you go up and your left side as you go down, and near the shore to avoid other boating traffic and the struggle against the wind.

Miles and Directions

0.0 Start by paddling up the Wailua River.

1.8 Look for a small opening with a large green dock on your right. This is Kamokila Hawaiian Village.

2.1 Paddle 0.35 miles past the Kamokila Hawaiian Village, turning right at the fork and landing on the beach.

Note: **The hiking measurements start from here. Hike upstream from the beach.**

0.15 The trail crosses the stream at a shallow spot.

0.35 Start walking on a boardwalk beside the stream.

0.82 Reach a cement tower beside the trail and stream.

0.92 Come to two stream crossings and a small waterfall, then the trail left turns away from the stream and goes up and over a hill.

1.12 The trail ends at the secret Uluwehi Falls. Enjoy the falls and pool before retracing your steps.

2.24 Arrive back at the beach and your kayak or SUP.

Uluwehi Falls (Secret Falls)

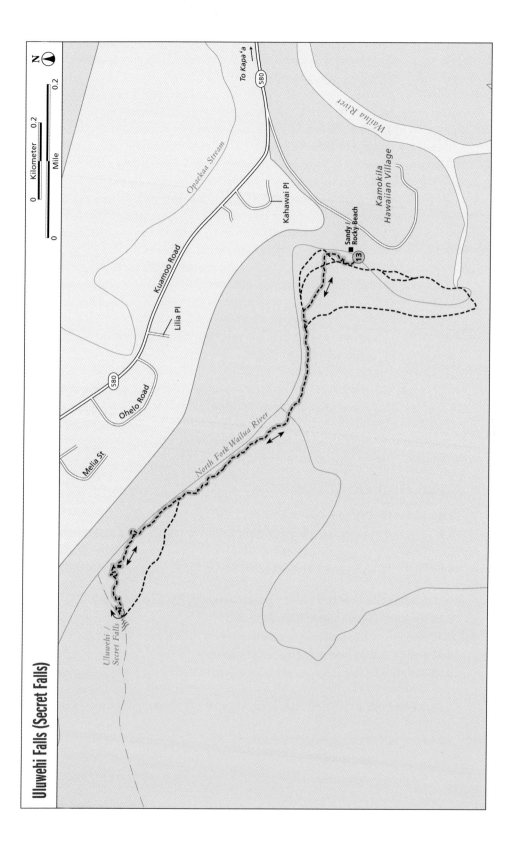

Kilometer 0 0.2

Mile 0 0.2

N

To Kapa'a
580

Opaekaa Stream

Kuamoo Road

Kahawai Pl

Lilia Pl

580

Ohelo Road

Melia St

North Fork Wailua River

Wailua River

Kamokila Hawaiian Village

Sandy / Rocky Beach

13

Uluwehi / Secret Falls

Additional Information

Call ahead for your kayak or stand-up paddleboard rental. There is spotty cell reception all over Kaua'i, and the various Wailua River outfitters sometimes sell out. A variety of outfitters and packages are available. I suggest doing a Google search and calling around in the middle of the day, Kaua'i time, as they may close early (e.g., one outfitter closes each day at 3 p.m.). Look for the outfitter with the right options for you and your crew. For example:

- Do you want a guided tour, or are you more adventurous?
- Do you want them to provide your lunch? Or do you prefer to bring your own?
- How much of a workout do you want? The winds and boat traffic often pick up in the afternoon, so going first thing in the morning may save you that upwind fight.
- How much sun do you want? It could be warmer and thus more comfortable swimming in the cool mountain stream water in the afternoon hours.
- Do you have to porter the SUP or kayak to the Wailua River, or will they deliver it for you? If so, is your vehicle prepared to do that?

Note: The Wailua River is closed for commercial traffic on Saturday and Sunday. The only outfitter who rents kayaks and SUPs on Sunday is Kamokila Hawaiian Village.

Here is a list of a few of the many Wailua River outfitters (find more online):

Kayak Wailua (808-822-3388; kayakwailua@gmail.com; https://kayakwailua .com). Guided kayak and hiking tours on a reservation basis, weather and river conditions permitting. Call for reservations between 7 a.m. and 9 p.m. Tours begin at 8 a.m., 9 a.m., 10 a.m., 11 a.m., 12 p.m., and 1 p.m. Check in 30 minutes prior to your tour time.

Scotty's Surf and Kayak (808-634-6982; scottyssurfco@gmail.com; https:// scottyssurfcokauai.com). Self-guided kayak, SUP, and surfboard rentals. Located in the Kapaa Sands Hotel. Open Monday through Friday from 9 a.m. to 3 p.m.

Rainbow Kayak Tours (866-826-2505 or 808-826-2505; rainbowkayak tours@gmail.com; https://rainbowkayak.com). Five- to 6-hour trips with lunch included. Tandem kayaks, paddles, back rests, and dry bags provided. Check in at the Snorkel Depot located behind Coconut Marketplace in the Aston Islander on the Beach Hotel parking area. Open Monday through Saturday with tours starting at 7 a.m. and 12:30 p.m.

14 Fern Grotto

Experience one of the greatest things to do on Kaua'i: paddle the Wailua River and hike to the fern grotto.

Height of falls: 50 feet
Type of falls: Free-falling plunge
Start: North Fork Wailua River. To reach this trail, you must first secure a kayak or stand-up paddleboard. See "Additional Information."
Distance: 0.5-mile round-trip hike plus anywhere from a 1-mile to 4.4-mile paddle, depending on where you launch
Difficulty: Easy trail, but the paddling makes it a full-body workout, especially in the afternoon when the trade winds are blowing in your face as you try to paddle down the river.
Hiking time: 30 minutes to 1 hour (depending on how long you view the beauty of this place)
Elevation change: 150 feet

Trail surface: Pavement and boardwalk
Wheelchair accessible: Yes
Seasons/schedule: Accessible year-round. Most outfitters require their boats returned by 4 or 5 p.m.
Fees and permits: None for the hike, but you may have to pay for your boat to get to the trailhead.
Land status: Public state park
Nearest town: Kapa'a
Other trail users: None
Canine compatibility: No
Water availability: Your outfitter may provide water for free or for a fee. Otherwise, there are large restrooms halfway up the trail.

Finding the trailhead: Just up the Wailua River, park at the launch, or arrive by shuttle, and kayak or SUP to the trailhead. The trailhead is a large rock and sand beach area on the North Fork Wailua River. Trailhead GPS: N22° 02.355', W159° 21.476'; Falls GPS: N22° 02.268', W159° 21.415'

The Hike

First, find an outfitter and rent a kayak or stand-up paddleboard. See "Additional Information." After paddling up the Wailua River 1.8 miles from the launch sites near Kuhio Highway / HI 56, you will have the option of getting out and exploring the Kamokila Hawaiian Village, or continuing your paddle trip up the Wailua River 0.2 miles and turning left at the fork (right takes you to Secret Falls), going a very short distance to a large dock with a platform with a green handrail. This is where the trailhead to Fern Grotto is located.

On Sunday there will likely be no other boats here, so you can dock anywhere along the platform. Other days you may have to dock at the far right of the platform or in the trees where it says to dock a kayak, which may have debris washing up from the river and be muddy. Note that tour guides for other groups, especially large boats, may not appreciate random kayakers tying up where they will be dropping off their many tourists, so try to utilize the kayak unloading area Monday through Saturday.

Top: You have arrived.
Bottom: Stay behind the rails.

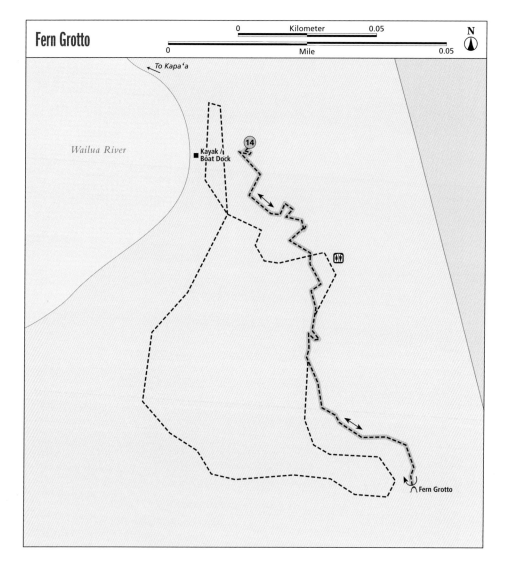

Once you are off your boat, you will see a large Wailua River State Park–Fern Grotto sign with massive yellow bamboo behind it. You will find large, fully functioning restrooms shortly into your hike.

Hike from your kayak approximately 0.5 mile along a wide, paved walkway through beautifully landscaped ferns, ginger, hau, and other rainforest plants to an awe-inspiring view of a massive cave covered in Boston sword ferns. There is a large platform to stand on while gazing up toward the thousands of ferns hanging all over the wall with a small waterfall often free-falling down from the middle of the cave's prominent roof. Take in the beauty of the various plants, the calmness of the flowing falls, and the Boston sword ferns that seem to cover every inch of the wall!

Note: Heed the warning signs and stay behind the railings and fences to respect this fragile area. Do not touch or feed the tropical birds or jungle fowl.

Miles and Directions

0.0 Start by paddling up the Wailua River.

0.20 Paddle 0.20 miles past Kamokila Village, turning left at the fork and landing at the large platform with green rails.

Note: **The hiking measurements start from here. Hike inland on a wide, paved walkway.**

0.25 Arrive at a large cave with a waterfall pouring over the center. Enjoy the views before retracing your steps.

0.5 Arrive back at the trailhead and paddle back down the Wailua River.

Gaze up at the falling waters and fern-covered walls.

Additional Information

Call ahead for your kayak or stand-up paddleboard rental. There is spotty cell reception all over Kaua'i, and the various Wailua River outfitters sometimes sell out. A variety of outfitters and packages are available. I suggest doing a Google search and calling around in the middle of the day, Kaua'i time, as they may close early (e.g., one outfitter closes each day at 3 p.m.). Look for the outfitter with the right options for you and your crew. For example:

- Do you want a guided tour, or are you more adventurous?
- Do you want them to provide your lunch? Or do you prefer to bring your own?
- How much of a workout do you want? The winds and boat traffic often pick up in the afternoon, so going first thing in the morning may save you that upwind fight.
- How much sun do you want? It could be warmer and thus more comfortable swimming in the cool mountain stream water in the afternoon hours.
- Do you have to porter the SUP or kayak to the Wailua River, or will they deliver it for you? If so, is your vehicle prepared to do that?

Note: The Wailua River is closed for commercial traffic on Sunday. The only outfitter who rents kayaks and SUPs on Sunday is Kamokila Hawaiian Village.

Here is a list of some of the Wailua River outfitters (find more online):

Kamokila Hawaiian Village (808-823-0559; villagekauai@gmail.com; http://villagekauai.com). Self-guided canoe rentals on a first-come, first-served basis. Reservations are recommended for groups of 10 or more and for guided outrigger canoe rides. Open daily 9 a.m. to 5 p.m., weather and river conditions permitting (summer hours, June 1 through August 31, are 8 a.m. to 7 p.m.).

Scotty's Surf and Kayak (808-634-6982; scottyssurfco@gmail.com; https://scottyssurfcokauai.com). Self-guided kayak, SUP, and surfboard rentals. Located in the Kapaa Sands Hotel. Open Monday through Friday from 9 a.m. to 3 p.m.

Rainbow Kayak Tours (866-826-2505 or 808-826-2505; rainbowkayaktours@gmail.com; https://rainbowkayak.com). Five- to 6-hour trips with lunch included. Tandem kayaks, paddles, back rests, and dry bags provided. Check in at the Snorkel Depot located behind Coconut Marketplace in the Aston Islander on the Beach Hotel parking area. Open Monday through Saturday with tours starting at 7 a.m. and 12:30 p.m.

15 Waipoʻo Falls

As you are driving up past Waimea Valley (aka "The Grand Canyon of the Pacific"), you can't help but see a huge waterfall flowing into the canyon at many different overlooks. That is Waipoʻo Falls!

Height of falls: 700 feet
Type of falls: Plunge
Start: Puʻu Hinahina Lookout
Distance: 2.86 miles out and back
Difficulty: Moderate
Hiking time: 1.5 to 2 hours (depending on how long you splash around and how many photos you take)
Elevation change: 800 feet
Trail surface: Slick rocks, roots, dirt, and mud

Seasons/schedule: Accessible year-round
Fees and permits: None
Land status: Public state park
Nearest town: Waimea
Other trail users: None
Canine compatibility: Yes, but must be on a leash
Water availability: Facilities at the trailhead/ parking lot

Finding the trailhead: Turn off HI 50 onto Waimea Canyon Drive/ HI 550. Drive 13.5 miles to a large parking lot for Waipoʻo Falls on your right (Halemary Road). The trailhead is at the back of the parking lot labeled "Puʻu Hinahina Parking." There is also a dirt parking lot down the four-wheel-drive Halemanu Road that can save you some hiking and a bit of time if you are in more of a hurry. Trailhead GPS: N22° 06.567', W159° 40.077'; Falls GPS: N22° 06.308', W159° 39.608'

The Hike

Start out in a grove of strawberry guava trees, descending switchbacks on a rooted, dirty trail for 0.42 mile. You will cross a small stream (which may not be flowing at all in the summer) and continue left up a heavily traveled trail. You'll cross more roots along your way through heavenly smelling ginger and strawberry guava as you head uphill.

You will top out at 0.55 mile and continue through the forest on a flat section of trail. There is a dirt parking lot on your left at 0.65 mile, but *do not* turn to go into the lot. Instead, continue straight until you reach 0.7 mile, where you can continue straight to go on the switchbacks down the hill or turn left to take a steeper way down. ***Note:*** I took the left fork, so the mileage may be a bit longer if you stay straight and go through the switchbacks here. You will go down a short, rooted section of trail, staying to your left.

You will pass through a nice native koa tree forest at 0.85 mile and then stay right at the intersection at 0.95 mile. Pass through a bunch of large boulders in the trail at 1.09 miles, watching your step, as it is sometimes narrow and steep. You will soon find a phenomenal 360-degree view at 1.2 miles that continues until 1.32 miles into the trail. You can see deep into Waimea Canyon and all the way to the ocean on a clear

Top: *A small falls before the big drop*
Bottom: *Stay at least 6 feet from the edge.*

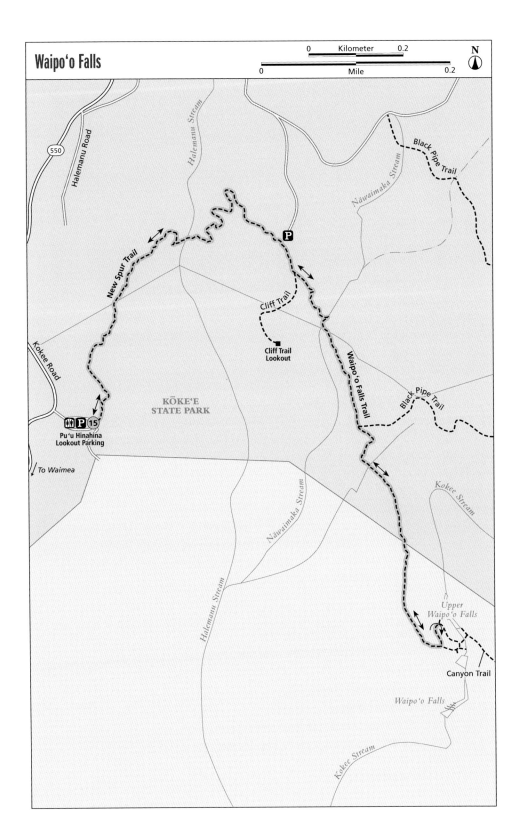

Waipo'o Falls

0   Kilometer   0.2

0   Mile   0.2

N

Halemanu Road

550

Halemanu Stream

Näwaimaka Stream

Black Pipe Trail

P

New Spur Trail

Cliff Trail

Cliff Trail Lookout

Kokee Road

Pu'u Hinahina Lookout Parking

P 15

To Waimea

KŌKE'E STATE PARK

Waipo'o Falls Trail

Black Pipe Trail

Näwaimaka Stream

Halemanu Stream

Kokee Stream

Upper Waipo'o Falls

Canyon Trail

Waipo'o Falls

Kokee Stream

Waipoʻo may be best seen from a roadside pull-off down the river.

day. Look out for the helicopters taking tourists to see Waipoʻo Falls and neat rock spires/outcroppings across the valley at 1.3 miles.

Turn left into the forest at 1.32 miles and then take the switchback right at 1.36 miles. Hike through some ginger and lantana with its yellow, orange, and pink flowers to arrive at the waterfall at 1.43 miles. Enjoy a cold soak at the small falls on your left. These small falls feed the enormous Waipoʻo Falls below the trail. Be very cautious if you attempt to look over to the falls, as there is no railing and the rocks and roots are very slick! *Caution:* There are no warning signs or ropes here to show you where a safe distance from the cliff edge is. Use caution when approaching the cliff, as the fall is hundreds of feet! Do not attempt to cross the stream if the water has covered all of the rocks or is brown, as this is a sign that flash flooding is occurring.

If you really want to get an expansive view of the entire 800-plus feet of waterfalls at Waipoʻo, I suggest you look for one of the many pull-offs along HI 550 / Kokee Road. Many of these pull-offs can be found as you drive back down Kokee Road, with the last one being Waimea Canyon Overlook.

Miles and Directions

0.0 Start at the large parking lot for Waipoʻo Falls.

0.42 Cross a streambed and continue up the other side.

0.55 Reach the ridgeline.

0.7 Go down some steep switchbacks.

0.95 Stay right at the intersection.

1.32 Turn left to stay in the forest and go down a switchback.

1.43 The trail ends at the top of Waipoʻo Falls. Enjoy the views and falls before retracing your steps.

2.86 Arrive back at the trailhead.

16 Red Dirt Waterfall

At a roadside pull–off near mile marker 23 off HI 550, you will see the stark contrast of bright white flowing water against Kaua'i's burnt sienna red dirt. Imagine you have been transported to America's Southwest for a minute while checking out Red Dirt Waterfall.

Height of falls: 15 feet
Type of falls: Plunge
Start: Waimea Canyon overlook near HI 550 mile marker 23
Distance: 100 feet each way
Difficulty: Easy
Hiking time: 15–30 minutes (depending on how long you take in the view)
Elevation change: 20 feet
Trail surface: Red dirt

Seasons/schedule: Accessible year-round
Fees and permits: None
Land status: Unknown, though most likely private
Nearest town: Waimea
Other trail users: None
Canine compatibility: Yes, but must be on a leash
Water availability: None

Finding the trailhead: Turn off HI 50 onto Waimea Canyon Drive. Drive 4.5 miles to the Waimea Canyon overlook on your right near mile marker 23 on HI 550. Walk across the road to the falls. Parking GPS: N22° 00.527', W159° 40.515'; Falls GPS: N22° 00.538', W159° 40.522'

The contrast of white on red is otherworldly.

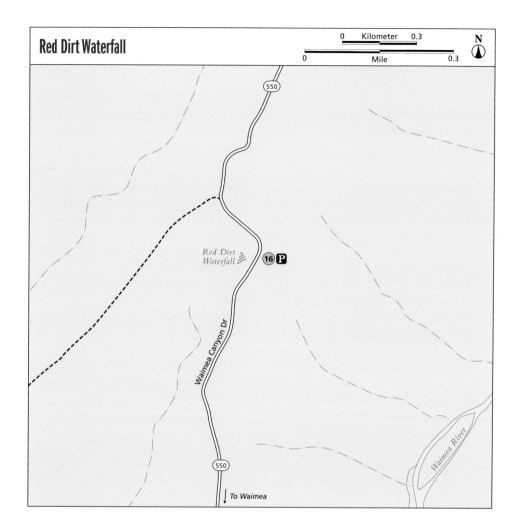

0   Kilometer   0.3

0   Mile   0.3

N

550

Red Dirt
Waterfall

16 P

Waimea Canyon Dr

Waimea River

550

To Waimea

The Hike

Called the Grand Canyon of the Pacific, Waimea Canyon is massive . . . and red.
Enjoy this Mars-like landscape by stopping at the various roadside pull-offs up HI
550 as it climbs along the side of Waimea Canyon. One of the first pull-offs you
come to is near mile marker 23 and provides views of Waimea Canyon on one side
and a seemingly out-of-place vibrantly white waterfall against the dark red dirt
ground on the other.

Park on the right at one of the roadside pull-offs, and hike from your car to
the waterfall across HI 550. Make sure to watch for other cars and keep your kids
and pets close to you, as this road can get busy and sometimes has speeding cars or
trucks.

Hike to the base of the falls or up the dirt path to the right of them if you want to see the view from the top. Back at your car, make sure to enjoy the overlook, looking down on Waimea Canyon, the Waimea River, and the town of Waimea below. After viewing the falls, you may want to continue up HI 550 to see the dramatic Nāpali Cliffs at Kōkeʻe State Park or the massive Waipoʻo Falls farther up Waimea Canyon.

Miles and Directions

More of a drive than a hike, walk across the road approximately 100 feet to the base of Red Dirt Waterfall. Make sure to take in the view of the expansive Waimea Canyon when looking down from the side of the road you parked on.

Maui Waterfalls

Home to another of the wettest spots on Earth, Big Bog, the streams off Haleakalā Crater flow about as good as any others in the Hawaiian islands. A drive along the Hana Highway reveals valley after valley, with waterfall after waterfall. You don't even need to get out of your car to see dozens of beautiful, flowing falls. If you do venture beyond the view from inside your glass windows, you will find some of the most epic falls tucked deep in these green canyons.

Driving east from the airport in Kahului, you will pass through the town of Paia before going on a windy road with sheer drops down to the coastline on your left and steep ridges on your right. Stop for some fresh fruit and a fun hike back to the many pools along the trail on your way to Twin Falls. Take another break at the Pua'a Ka'a State Wayside to enjoy a lunch at one of the many picnic tables while listening to the falls flowing all around you.

Take a quick stretch of the legs with a hike and swim at Wailua Falls. Then finish your day at the Kīpahulu Visitor Center at Haleakalā National Park, where you find the Seven Sacred Pools, Waimoku Falls, and Makahiku Falls. Plan to camp at Kīpahulu Campground, stay at one of the hotels in Hana, double-back to Paia, or finish your loop around Haleakalā by driving the road around the dry south side of Haleakalā Crater. Your trip will be filled with jaw-dropping sights and a variety of waterfalls.

17 Makahiku Falls

From the 'Ohe'o Gulch trailhead at the Kīpahulu Visitor Center at Haleakalā National Park, you can walk just a little over half a mile to a lookout with views of a stunning gorge and a 200-foot-tall waterfall.

Height of falls: 200 feet
Type of falls: Horsetail
Start: Kīpahulu Visitor Center, Haleakalā National Park
Distance: 1.16 miles out and back
Difficulty: Easy
Hiking time: About 1 hour
Elevation change: 300 feet
Trail surface: Wide dirt path
Seasons/schedule: Accessible year-round. Open 9 a.m. to 5 p.m. daily. The parking lot closes at 5 p.m., so make sure to be out prior to that.

Fees and permits: Park entrance fee
Land status: National park
Nearest town: Hana
Other trail users: Those camping at Kīpahulu Campground and many park visitors
Canine compatibility: No, dogs are only allowed on the paved areas and not on the trails.
Water availability: Water fountains at the parking lot restrooms. Stream water at the falls, which must be purified due to the risk of leptospirosis throughout the Hawai'i islands.

Finding the trailhead: From the intersection of the Hana Highway and Keawa Place in the seaside town of Hana, drive 10 miles south on HI 360 / Hana Highway to the Kīpahulu Visitor Center in the Kīpahulu District of Haleakalā National Park. There is ample parking, along with restrooms and the nearby Kīpahulu Campground. Walk *mauka* (toward the mountains) on the wide Pipiwai Trail. Make sure to stay on the trail and watch for traffic crossing the street. Trailhead GPS: N20° 39.705', W156° 02.602'; Falls GPS: N20° 39.911', W156° 02.900'

The Hike

From the parking lot you will walk a paved path uphill to where the trail splits, with the Pipiwai Trail going up to the left and across the Hana Highway, and the Kūloa Point Trail going downhill to the right. Take the Pipiwai Trail to the left and continue approximately 0.5 mile on a flat roadbed with a gradual incline until you see a Haleakalā National Park interpretive sign on your right that identifies Makahiku Falls. You can look past the sign into the deep, green valley below where the waterfall creates a wedding veil shape as it plunges into the valley.

Makahiku refers to the cathedral-like cliffs that surround this valley-eroding waterfall. Make sure to enjoy it at a distance, as Hawai'i's steep canyon walls are notorious for loose rocks falling down without warning or provocation. Enjoy the shade as you look out onto this sun-drenched waterfall and the cathedral walls that surround it. You may then want to continue your journey deeper into the valley, and farther up the Pipiwai Trail, to Waimoku Falls.

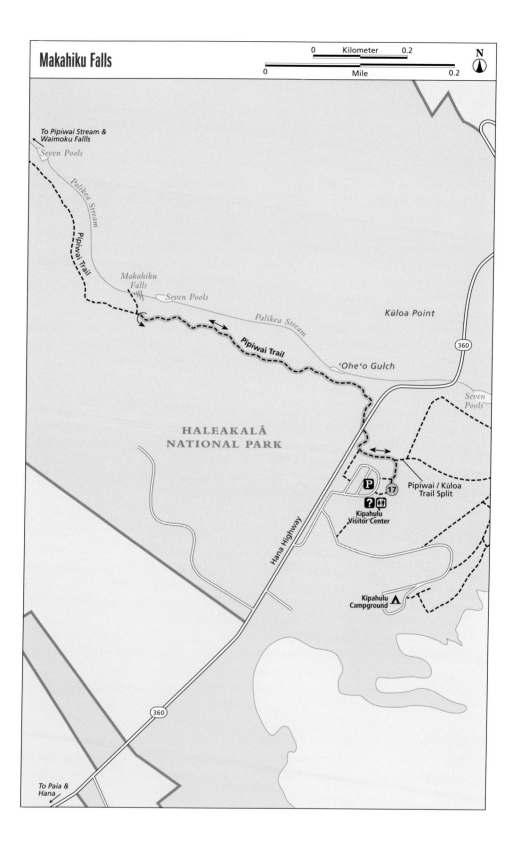

Makahiku Falls

0   Kilometer   0.2

0   Mile   0.2

N

To Pipiwai Stream &
Waimoku Fallls

Seven Pools

Palikea Stream

Pipiwai Trail

*Makahiku
Falls*

Seven Pools

Palikea Stream

Kūloa Point

Pipiwai Trail

'Ohe'o Gulch

360

*Seven
Pools*

HALEAKALĀ
NATIONAL PARK

P

17

Pipiwai / Kūloa
Trail Split

? 🚻

Kipahulu
Visitor Center

Kipahulu
Campground △

Hana Highway

360

To Paia &
Hana

Clearings expose more of Makahiku Falls. CINJA STRICKLAND

See the top of Makahiku Falls from the Pipiwai Trail. CINJA STRICKLAND

Most of the trail is shaded by tree canopies, but the path is wide and open in sections, so be sure to wear sunscreen or skin-covering clothes to protect from the intense sun exposure.

Miles and Directions

0.0 Start hiking the Pipiwai Trail from Kīpahulu Visitor Center.

0.08 Follow the Pipiwai Trail across the Hana Highway.

0.58 Reach the Makahiku Falls overlook. Enjoy the views before retracing your steps.

1.16 Arrive back at the trailhead.

Additional Information

This land, and much of upcountry Maui, is owned by US National Park System, so you must obtain a permit to adventure here. Permits are valid for three days, are good at both the summit of Haleakalā and Kīpahulu Areas of Haleakalā National Park. Fees and permits for entry into the Haleakalā National Park vary depending on whether you are going in as an individual, bicycling in, riding a motorcycle, driving a car, or going as a group. Annual passes are also available.

Pay the national park entry fee via credit card upon entry at the Kīpahulu Visitor Center parking lot. The Kīpahulu Visitor Center office can be contacted through www.nps .gov/hale/planyourvisit/kipahulu.htm or by phone at (808) 293-9201. You can also reach the Haleakalā National Park office at (808) 572-4400.

18 Waimoku Falls

From the 'Ohe'o Gulch trailhead at the Kīpahulu Visitor Center at Haleakalā National Park, you can walk past the Makahiku Falls overlook on a very well marked and maintained trail to a massive 400-foot-tall waterfall cascading down a wide wall.

Height of falls: 400 feet
Type of falls: Plunge
Start: Kīpahulu Visitor Center, Kīpahulu National Park
Distance: 3.8 miles out and back
Difficulty: Moderate
Hiking time: About 2 hours (depending on how many pictures and stops you take)
Elevation change: 900 feet
Trail surface: Wide dirt path with a few rocky spots to be careful on while traversing
Seasons/schedule: Accessible year-round. Open 9 a.m. to 5 p.m. daily. The parking lot closes at 5 p.m., so make sure to be out prior to that.
Fees and permits: Park entrance fee
Land status: National park
Nearest town: Hana
Other trail users: Those camping at Kīpahulu Campground and many park visitors
Canine compatibility: No, dogs are only allowed on the paved areas and not on the trails.
Water availability: Water fountains at the parking lot restrooms. Stream water at the falls, which must be purified due to the risk of leptospirosis throughout the Hawai'i islands.

Finding the trailhead: Take HI 360 / Hana Highway 10.4 miles to the Kīpahulu Visitor Center and start walking *mauka* (toward the mountains) on the wide trail. Watch for traffic crossing the street. Trailhead GPS: N20° 39.705', W156° 02.602'; Falls GPS: N20° 40.695', W156° 03.310'

The Hike

From the parking lot you will walk a paved path uphill to where the trail splits, with the Pipiwai Trail going up to the left and across the Hana Highway, and the Kūloa Point Trail going downhill to the right. Take the Pipiwai Trail to the left and continue approximately 0.5 mile on a flat roadbed with a gradual incline until you see a Haleakalā National Park interpretive sign on your right that identifies Makahiku Falls. Take a peak at Makahiku Falls and then continue up the valley trail toward Waimoku Falls.

At 0.7 mile into the hike the trail will circle around a large mango tree. Then at 0.8 mile you will stand under a huge, wide-reaching banyan tree that evokes thoughts of the one that takes up an entire city block in downtown Lahaina! Many people stop in awe of this massive beast of a tree, take group photos under it, or be tempted to climb into it. Please fight the urge to climb on this natural wonder so that future generations will also be able to enjoy it.

Some nice pools and falls will be on your right at 0.9 mile and then there will be two bridges that overlook a network of small falls and pools at 1.2 miles. Shortly after

Left: Enjoy the shaded boardwalk. CINJA STRICKLAND
Right: From bamboo to bridges. CINJA STRICKLAND

the bridges across the gulch, you will walk into a bamboo forest. A wide, elevated boardwalk will carry you through the thick, dark bamboo, some of which reach heights of over 40 feet tall. Walk in wonder and amazement as you journey through this thicket of bamboo, which is a type of grass. Let your "Honey I Shrunk the Kids" mind run free as you cross out of the deep grass into an opening in the forest that gives you the first glimpse of Waimoku Falls at 1.9 miles.

At 400 feet tall, Waimoku Falls has a commanding stature. Dwarfing all of the trees below, its cascades appear to fall from the heavens as you get closer and closer to it. If the conditions are right, and they often are here, a second waterfall can be seen flowing from the canyon to the left of Waimoku Falls.

Waimoku can mean water that cuts, severs, amputates, or breaks in two. And one sees just how this waterfall is cutting into the mountain it flows from. Enjoy the view from a distance, as the water cutting into the mountain also frees rocks from the cliff sides high above, bringing them crashing down. Canyoneers will tell you that when a rock dislodges from the face of a waterfall, it can kick out away from the face of the falls just as far as the height it is falling from. So, based on that logic, a rock could fall as far as 400 feet out from the face of Waimoku Falls! Stand back and enjoy its beauty safely. Please honor the sign that says "Do Not Pass This Point—Fatalities Have Occurred." We want you to come back many more times.

Pools and falls everywhere! CINJA STRICKLAND

The Pipiwai Trail ends with a beautiful view of Waimoku Falls. CINJA STRICKLAND

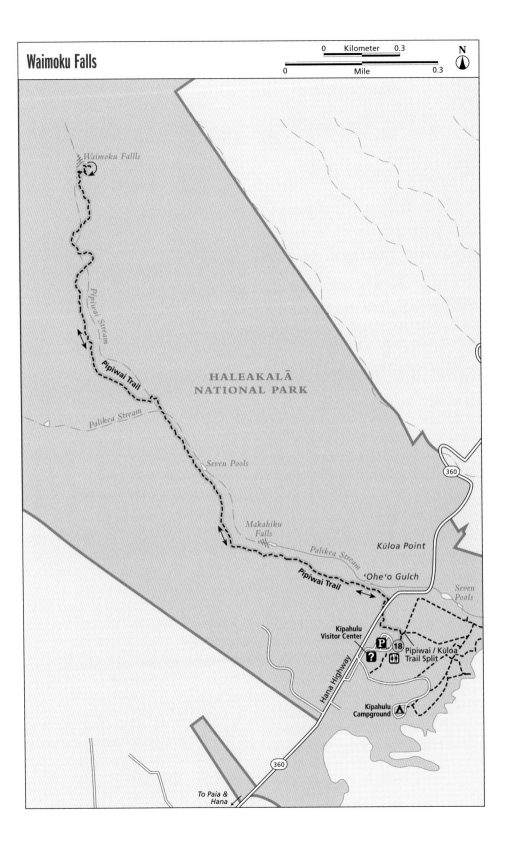

Waimoku Falls

0 Kilometer 0.3
0 Mile 0.3

N

Waimoku Fallls

Pipiwai Stream

Pipiwai Trail

HALEAKALĀ
NATIONAL PARK

Palikea Stream

Seven Pools

Makahiku
Falls

Palikea Stream

Kūloa Point

'Oheʻo Gulch

Pipiwai Trail

Seven
Pools

360

Kīpahulu
Visitor Center

18

Pipiwai / Kūloa
Trail Split

Hana Highway

Kīpahulu
Campground

360

To Paia &
Hana

Left: Cross two bridges along the way. CINJA STRICKLAND
Right: So much water! CINJA STRICKLAND

Miles and Directions

0.0 Start hiking the Pipiwai Trail from Kīpahulu Visitor Center

0.08 Follow the Pipiwai Trail across the Hana Highway.

0.58 Reach the Makahiku Falls overlook.

0.8 Pass under a huge banyan tree.

1.2 Cross two bridges that overlook a network of small falls and pools.

1.9 The trail ends at an observation point. Enjoy the view of Waimoku Falls before retracing your steps.

3.8 Arrive back at the trailhead.

Additional Information

Permits are required. As part of the National Park system, Haleakalā National Park provides access at the same rates as those on the mainland. If you have a National Parks Pass, then it will work here to get your vehicle in at no charge. Permits are valid for three days, are good at both the summit of Haleakalā and Kīpahulu Areas of Haleakalā National Park. Fees and permits for entry into the Haleakalā National Park vary depending on whether you are going in as an individual, bicycling in, riding a motorcycle, driving a car, or going as a group.

Pay the National Park entry fee via credit card upon entry of the Kīpahulu Visitor Center parking lot. The office is open, and they can be communicated with through https://www.nps.gov/hale/planyourvisit/kipahulu.htm or by calling the Kīpahulu Visitor Center at (808) 293-9201. You can also reach the Haleakalā National Park office at (808) 572-4400.

19 'Ohe'o Pools (Seven Sacred Pools)

From the 'Ohe'o Gulch trailhead at the Kīpahulu Visitor Center at Haleakalā National Park, you can walk *makai* (toward the ocean) on a very well marked and maintained trail to seven plunge pools that fill from waterfalls flowing from below the Hana Highway all the way into the ocean.

Height of falls: Varying heights
Type of falls: Segment
Start: Kīpahulu Visitor Center, Haleakalā National Park
Distance: 0.56-mile loop
Difficulty: Easy, but beware of slick rocks, steep cliffs, and flash floods.
Hiking time: About 30 minutes (depending on how many photos you take at the pools and coast)
Elevation change: 115 feet
Trail surface: Mostly pavement and paved stairs, with some dirt path sections through the wooded areas

Seasons/schedule: Accessible year-round. Open 9 a.m. to 5 p.m. daily. The parking lot closes at 5 p.m., so make sure to be out prior to that.
Fees and permits: Park entrance fee
Land status: National park
Nearest town: Hana
Other trail users: Those camping at Kīpahulu Campground and coastal hikers
Canine compatibility: No, dogs are only allowed on the paved areas and not on the trails.
Water availability: Water fountains at the parking lot restrooms

Finding the trailhead: Take HI 360 / Hana Highway 10.4 miles to the Kīpahulu Visitor Center and start walking *mauka* (toward the mountains) on the wide Pipiwai Trail. Turn right at the junction to go down the Kūloa Point Trail to the 'Ohe'o Pools, coastal views, and archaeological sites. Trailhead GPS: N20° 39.705', W156° 02.602'; Falls GPS: N20° 39.803', W156° 02.486'

The Hike

From the parking lot you will walk a paved path uphill to where the trail splits, with the Pipiwai Trail going up to the left and across the Hana Highway, and the Kūloa Point Trail going downhill to the right. Take the Kūloa Point Trail to the right and continue on the right fork of this trail so that you will do the Kūloa Point Trail counterclockwise.

After approximately 0.25 mile downhill on the paved pathway, you will come to a picturesque viewpoint looking up the valley to a bridge across the Hana Highway with the stream proceeding down to multiple waterfalls cascading from pool to pool all the way to the ocean below. You will enjoy various viewpoints over the ocean and along the stream.

Hike out to the end of Kūloa Point, checking out the jagged cliffs and arches carved by the sea just below you. The Kahakai Trail offers a side hike of 0.3 mile along the coast to the Kīpahulu Campground. Stay on the Kūloa Point Trail back up the

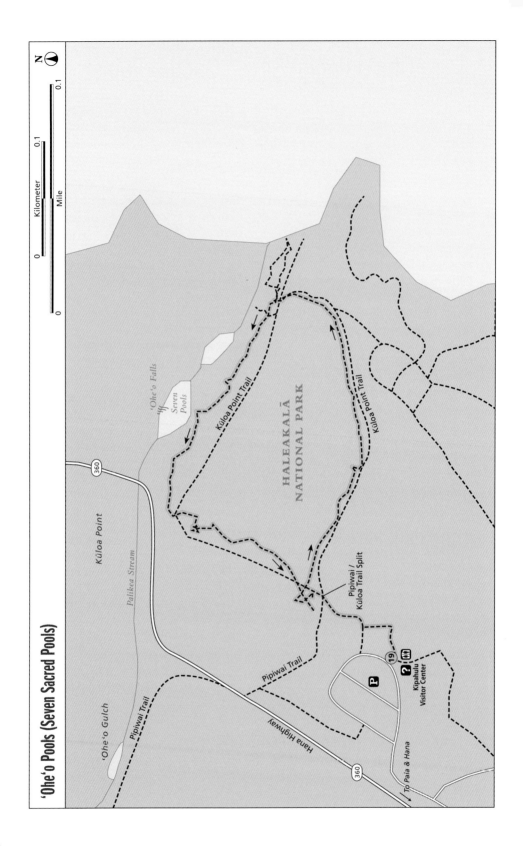

'Ohe'o Pools (Seven Sacred Pools)

N

Kilometer
0   0.1   0.1

Mile
0   0.1   0.1

Kūloa Point

Palikea Stream

'Ohe'o Gulch

'Ohe'o Falls

Seven Pools

360

Pipiwai Trail

Kūloa Point Trail

Kūloa Point Trail

HALEAKALĀ NATIONAL PARK

Pipiwai / Kūloa Trail Split

Pipiwai Trail

Hana Highway

P

19

Kipahulu Visitor Center

To Paia & Hana

360

From the mountains to the ocean

canyon via some well-maintained stairs to see all seven of the sacred pools up to the bridge under the Hana Highway. There the trail turns back to the right, leaving the stream and going through the forest back toward the parking lot.

Enjoy a history lesson of some of the local culture through the interpretive signs along the way back, which tell of the history of the rock foundations you see here. They were the home site of the Po'onika family, who received this land in 1848 when Hawai'i's lands were first divided by King Kamehameha III. Prior to that no one could own land in Hawai'i! Lands were divided by King Kamehameha III among the king, chiefs, and the Hawaiian Kingdom's government. Land parcels, called Land Commission Awards, were granted to common people who met certain narrow criteria. The Po'onika family received this parcel from the king.

Miles and Directions

0.0 Start hiking the Pipiwai Trail from the Kīpahulu Visitor Center

0.08 Turn right onto the Kūloa Point Trail. Do not cross the Hana Highway. Continue on the Kūloa Point Trail to your right to do the loop counterclockwise.

0.25 Reach Palikea Stream and an 'Ohe'o Pools overlook. Venture down to the coast and then hike back up to continue on the loop.

0.56 Arrive back at the trailhead.

Additional Information

Permits are required. As part of the National Park system, Haleakalā National Park provides access at the same rates as those on the mainland. If you have a National Parks Pass, then it will work here to get your vehicle in at no charge. Permits are valid for three days, are good at both the summit of Haleakalā and Kīpahulu Areas of Haleakalā National Park. Fees and permits for entry into the Haleakalā National Park vary depending on whether you are going in as an individual, bicycling in, riding a motorcycle, driving a car, or going as a group.

Pay the National Park entry fee via credit card upon entry of the Kīpahulu Visitor Center parking lot. The office is open, and they can be communicated with through https://www.nps.gov/hale/planyourvisit/kipahulu.htm or by calling the Kīpahulu Visitor Center at (808) 293-9201. You can also reach the Haleakalā National Park office at (808) 572-4400.

20 Wailua Falls

After mile marker 44 (and almost to mile marker 45) on the Hana Highway heading south from Hana, you can walk a very short distance to a roadside waterfall with a swimming pool. The parking lot is small. Do not stop here if there is no parking—there are plenty of waterfalls and parking just a bit farther at 'Ohe'o Gulch.

Height of falls: 80 feet
Type of falls: Plunge
Start: Parking lot at mile marker 44.8 on the Hana Highway
Distance: 0.2 mile out and back
Difficulty: Easy, but beware of slick rocks, steep cliffs, and flash floods.
Hiking time: About 10 minutes (not counting time swimming in the pool or taking pictures)
Elevation change: 10 feet
Trail surface: Slick rocks and roots at the base of waterfall

Seasons/schedule: Accessible year-round
Fees and permits: None
Land status: Ko'olau Forest Reserve
Nearest town: Hana
Other trail users: Lots of looky-loo tourists snarling up traffic along the Hana Highway
Canine compatibility: Yes
Water availability: Stream water at the falls, which must be purified due to the risk of leptospirosis throughout the Hawai'i islands

Finding the trailhead: Park in the little (8 to 10 cars) parking lot at mile 44.8 on the Hana Highway / HI 360 and walk across the bridge to the north/east side of Honolewa Stream. Look for a faint trail on the right side of the stream as you look from the bridge toward the falls. Trailhead GPS: N20° 40.990', W156° 01.731'; Falls GPS: N20° 41.004', W156° 01.764'

The Hike

From the small (8 to 10 cars) parking lot, you will walk across the bridge to the trailhead. Go up the short, rugged trail approximately 50 feet to the base of the 80-foot-tall cascading waterfall with a wide and relatively deep swimming pool. Jump in and cool off for a bit before heading on your way along the Hana Highway.

Do not stop on the Hana Highway if the parking lot is full. Continue on to the Seven Sacred Pools, Waimoku Falls, 'Ohe'o Gulch, and so forth, where there is much more parking and even more beautiful waterfalls and pools.

You can even prepare for the upcoming, very accessible parking lot to be full by having the passenger of your car ready with a camera to snap some quick pics at mile marker 44 as you drive by Wailua Falls around 44.8 miles along the Hana Highway when coming from Kahului. If you are lucky enough to snag a parking spot, be very careful crossing the road to the falls. *Do not* walk in the road or tie up traffic any more than is absolutely necessary.

If you make it to the falls, have your swimsuit on for a not-too-cold dip in the crystal-clear mountain water that flows down from Honolewa Stream. Watch for

Even the view from the road is great!

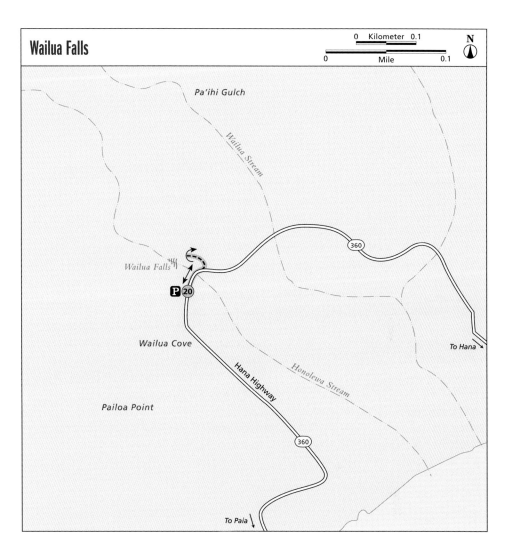

falling rocks and local cliff divers as you float or swim around. If the water starts to turn brown, turn around. Flash floods are a real risk here.

Miles and Directions

0.0 Start from the small parking lot past mile marker 44 on the Hana Highway.

0.1 Walk across the bridge and go up the short, rugged trail to the right of the stream to reach the waterfall.

0.2 Arrive back at the trailhead.

21 Pua'a Ka'a Falls

Just about a half mile along the Hana Highway past mile marker 22, you can stop at the roadside Pua'a Ka'a State Wayside and take a short stroll to a few waterfalls and plunge pools on a very well marked and maintained trail.

Height of falls: 15 feet and 25 feet
Type of falls: Plunge
Start: Pua'a Ka'a State Wayside near mile marker 22.5 on the Hana Highway
Distance: 0.24 mile out and back
Difficulty: Easy, but beware of slick rocks, rocks falling from cliffs, and flash floods. Don't get near the river if it is flooding (i.e., looking brown).
Hiking time: About 20 minutes (depending on whether you have a picnic and how many pools you swim in)
Elevation change: 110 feet
Trail surface: Paved
Wheelchair accessible: Yes

Seasons/schedule: Accessible year-round. Open dawn to dusk daily.
Fees and permits: None
Land status: State of Hawai'i
Nearest town: Hana
Other trail users: Those looking to stretch their legs while driving the long and windy Hana Highway
Canine compatibility: Yes
Water availability: Sinks are available at this state wayside. There will likely be no soap. Newly renovated restrooms were available as of the time of this writing. Please do your best to maintain them to keep them open to the public.

Finding the trailhead: Park at the Pua'a Ka'a State Wayside near mile 22.5 of the Hana Highway / HI 360, approximately 39 miles east of Kahului or 11.7 miles west of Hana. If the main parking lot is full, please continue on so as not to back up traffic along the Hana Highway. The trail starts right across the street. Trailhead GPS: N20° 49.012', W156° 07.416'; Falls GPS: N20° 48.976', W156° 07.453'

The Hike

Pua'a Ka'a State Wayside is a great spot to stretch your legs, enjoy a picnic lunch, or take a swim. After just a few hundred feet of leisurely strolling along a mostly flat trail, you can enjoy a peaceful roadside respite. Let the sounds of the falling waters and singing birds drown your worries and the stresses of driving the Hana Highway.

Immediately after you cross the road, you will be greeted by a short, 15-foot-tall cascading falls with a small pool worthy of a quick dip. Continue up the trail, past the four covered picnic tables, to the larger 25-foot-tall waterfall with its nice, big swimming pool. From a lookout to the right of the trailhead, you can frame both waterfalls and pools nicely into a photo.

Pack a picnic lunch and plan ahead to enjoy one of the many covered picnic tables. Make sure to wear your swimsuit to enjoy swimming around, under, and even behind the falling water of Pua'a Ka'a Falls. Be very cautious about the slick, and

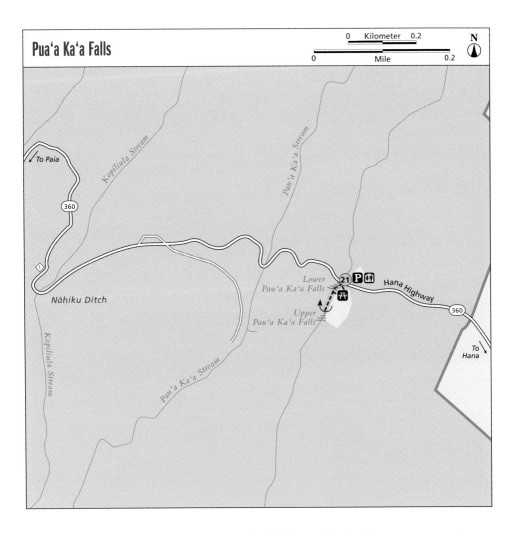

Pua'a Ka'a Falls

often sharp, rocks. The rocks move and roll often in the flowing water, so watch your step and double-check the depth of the pool before you attempt to jump in.

Miles and Directions

0.0 Start at the Pua'a Ka'a State Wayside near mile 22.5 of the Hana Highway.

0.12 Walk across the road to arrive at two small waterfalls and their pools. Enjoy a picnic or swim before retracing your steps.

0.24 Cross the Hana Highway to arrive back at the wayside.

Turn page: Flowing falls and pools welcome ▶
weary travelers. CINJA STRICKLAND

22 Twin Falls

From the large surfboard sign announcing Twin Falls alongside the Hana Highway at mile marker 2, you can hike to many waterfalls and plunge pools on a very well marked and maintained trail.

Height of falls: 40 feet
Type of falls: Plunge
Start: Parking lot at mile marker 2 on the Hana Highway
Distance: 1.9 miles out and back
Difficulty: Moderate, but beware of slick rocks, rocks falling from cliffs, and flash floods. Don't cross the river if it is flooding (i.e., looking brown).
Hiking time: About 1 hour (depending on how many pools you swim in)
Elevation change: 188 feet
Trail surface: Mostly gravel and dirt roads
Seasons/schedule: Accessible year-round. Open 8 a.m. to 4 p.m. daily.

Fees and permits: Donations encouraged
Land status: Private land (Wailele Farm)
Nearest town: Paia
Other trail users: Those looking to stretch their legs while driving the long and windy Hana Highway
Canine compatibility: Yes
Water availability: Stream water at the falls, which must be purified due to the risk of leptospirosis throughout the Hawai'i islands
Other: Bring cash for the Twin Falls Farmstand, which sells local fruit, coconuts, smoothies, and snacks. Porta-johns are located 500 feet up the trail. Please leave a tip to keep them open to the public.

Finding the trailhead: Park on the roadside of the Hana Highway / HI 360 11.6 miles south of Paia on your right on the way toward Hana. If the main parking lot is full, you can continue just a bit farther down the road toward Hana to find additional parking. The trail starts right beside the bright yellow and blue surfboard that says "Twin Falls" in bold red letters. Trailhead GPS: N20° 54.721', W156° 14.492'; Falls GPS: N20° 54.168', W156° 14.430'

The Hike

This private farm is open to the public for hiking and swimming! From the parking lot you will pass by the big yellow surfboard and start your journey into the valley. There is a wide variety of tropical flowers along the wide, gravel road hike. Stay to the left at the three-way intersection.

The farm is a working farm, so be on the lookout for bananas ripening high in the trees or pineapples fruiting on the bushes along the trail. *Do not pick the fruit!* Unless you have recently been hired as a farmer here, the fruit you see in the trees is not made for you to pick.

After approximately 0.2 mile of a pretty flat pathway, you will come to a picturesque viewpoint looking down on a short waterfall cascading into a large turquoise swimming pool. The wide rock beach will beckon you to traverse down the slick trail to the creek bed and walk up the creek a short distance to play in the pool. Whether you are frolicking in the cool, clear water or jumping off the waterfall face, be very cautious about the slick, and often sharp, rocks. The rocks move and roll often in the flowing water, so double-check the depth of the pool before you attempt to jump in.

Continue up the trail, farther into the valley, until it comes to a peak as a single-track trail at approximately 0.7 mile in. The trail then opens back up a bit and declines to the streambed. There are two stream crossings at 0.8 mile. Do not attempt to cross the stream if it is flowing stronger than you feel comfortable. Definitely do not ever attempt to cross a flash-flooding stream. You can tell a stream is flash flooding when the water has turned brown or is carrying debris in it. The brown sediment and debris (sticks, etc.) tend to dislodge from a stream's banks when the water is higher than its average depth.

The second stream crossing looks to be an old dam, likely used during Maui's sugarcane days. Either ford the stream (safest method) or hike across the dam to a set of old stairs off the back side. Hike up the stream until you reach a very large swimming pool and beautiful fern grotto framing a gorgeous waterfall that flows out into

Pretty pools to swim in

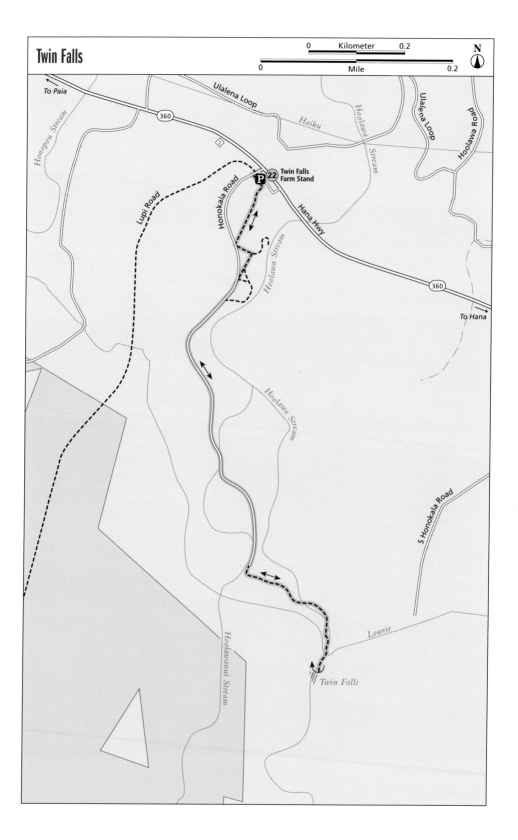

Twin Falls

0   Kilometer   0.2

0   Mile   0.2

N

To Paia

Ulalena Loop

360

Haiku

Hoolawa

Ulalena Loop

Hoolawa Road

Honopou Stream

Hoolawa Stream

2

Honokala Road

P 22 Twin Falls Farm Stand

Hana Hwy

Lupi Road

Hoolawa Stream

360

To Hana

Hoolawa Stream

S Honokala Road

Lowrie

Hoolawanui Stream

Twin Falls

Twins? Nandor Szotak

The main pool has room to swim around.

the middle of the deep pool. A closer look reveals two waterfalls flowing side by side, thus living up to the name Twin Falls. You could spend most of the day here—taking in the view, swimming laps around the falling water as it plunges into the center of the large pool, or soaking up the sun on the rocks while you watch the daring cliff divers practice their tricks.

Enjoy a history lesson on some of the local culture and learn about what all is going on in this valley by taking a Wailele Farm tour. They tell how "[t]he Koʻolau rainforest, which feeds the two Hoʻolawa streams running through our farm, is filled with fresh water year-round. On average there is 80–100 inches of rain per year in this rainforest. This freshwater provides ideal growing conditions for an abundance of plant life. Contained within this valley is all that is necessary for sustainability; fertile soil, fresh water, and sunlight." Check out www.twinfallsmaui.net for more information. They can also be contacted by phone at (808) 463-1275 (text preferred).

Miles and Directions

0.0 Start at the large parking lot at mile marker 2 on the Hana Highway.

0.2 Hike past the big yellow surfboard and porta-johns, then look for some pools and falls to your left.

0.8 Make two stream crossings, the second of which is at an old dam.

0.95 The trail ends at Twin Falls. Enjoy the pool and views before retracing your steps.

1.9 Arrive back at the trailhead.

O'ahu Waterfalls

O'ahu is known as "The Gathering Place." That moniker is no different when it comes to waterfalls. Home to the most waterfalls of any island in this book, the variety and beauty of the falls found on O'ahu show that they all seem to gather here. From short and wide block falls to very tall plunge falls, they can all be found here.

Within both the Waianae Mountains and the Ko'olau Mountain Range lie some of the most serene and idyllic mountain streams. Just a few minutes drive from the hustle of Waikiki, you can be transported back in time to the same waterfalls locals enjoyed over a hundred years ago. Side by side on a map, the streams of Manoa Valley and Nu'uanu Valley are fed from the highest peaks on the east/windward side of O'ahu. They both boast many streams and waterfalls flowing through them.

Get out there! Don't just stay within the Ala Wai channel confines of Waikiki. Venture out to the Hawai'i Nature Center, Lyon Arboretum, Waimea Valley, or the cute coastal town of La'ie. Make sure to see the beaches of the North Shore, the verdant Central Valley, and the sun-kissed Waianae Coast. Take a short stroll to Kapena Falls or Likeke Falls, or jump into the pools of Maunawili Falls or Waimano Falls. This island has it all!

I call O'ahu "Adventure Island," as it seems to have an adventure perfect for everyone who visits. Whether you prefer horseback riding, zip-lining, cliff diving, or just relaxing beside a babbling brook or on a remote beach, it's all here. Bring your hiking boots and swimsuit and be ready to journey deep into the ancient rainforests and swim in the pools. I have explored O'ahu's ridges and gulches for over eight years now, and still have barely scratched the surface of what amazing adventures await me here.

Make sure to plan some hikes and adventures into your trip to O'ahu. You'll be glad that you got out there and got to see some of the true ancient Hawai'i you've always heard and dreamt of.

23 Waimea Falls

In the back of Waimea Valley, just up from Waimea Bay and all of the fun of its massive wave competitions, bouldering, and cliff diving, is a quiet and serene botanical garden with a large waterfall that flows year-round. Stay along the main paved trail for 1 mile to arrive at the 45-foot tall falls and large pool.

Height of falls: 45 feet
Type of falls: Fan
Start: Waimea Valley botanical gardens ticket office
Distance: 2.2 miles out and back
Difficulty: Easy
Hiking time: 1.5 to 2 hours (depending on how long you wander through the gardens and stay at the pool)
Elevation change: 130 feet
Trail surface: Wide paved path
Wheelchair accessible: Yes

Seasons/schedule: Accessible year-round. The park is closed on Thanksgiving and Christmas Day.
Fees and permits: Entrance fee
Drone usage: Not allowed in the valley
Land status: Private land (Waimea Valley, owned and managed by Hi'ipaka LLC)
Nearest town: Waimea
Other trail users: None
Canine compatibility: No, except for service dogs
Water availability: Lots of fountains, snack bars, and restrooms

Finding the trailhead: Take Kamehameha Highway / HI 83 east 4.5 miles from Haleiwa and turn right on Waimea Valley Road. Park at the Waimea Valley botanical gardens. Make sure to tell the parking attendant you are going to the botanical gardens so you don't get charged for parking to go to the beach at Waimea Bay. At the time of this writing, there was no fee for parking to go to the botanical gardens! Cheehoo! Trailhead GPS: N21° 38.140', W158° 03.190'; Falls GPS: N21° 37.828', W158° 02.555'

The Hike

A large, heavy-flowing waterfall dropping into a big swimming pool in the back of a beautiful valley full of all kinds of flowers and trees! What could be better? It's cool to see a place where so many movies have been filmed. Walking into the park you see a row of movie posters for such films as Disney's *George of the Jungle*; *You, Me and Dupree*; and *The Hunger Games: Catching Fire*. This place has a storied past too. The park used to provide informative shows with cliff divers! Imagine them diving from the top of the falls when you see it firsthand.

Start at the entrance building and follow the wide main trail toward the back of the valley. You will cross a bridge at 0.15 mile and see the Hale Kipa on your left at 0.2 mile. Enjoy a large banyan tree on your right at 0.4 mile. Listen for the whirling windmill above as you pass a large grassy field on your right at 0.64 mile, then turn left and follow the main trail down the hill.

Be sure to look up the stream from the bridge at 0.94 mile.

Cross another bridge at 0.85 mile. Look for bananas in the middle of the stream on your left. Just across the bridge you find a shuttle stop with a snack bar serving ice cream, sodas, shave ice, and small snacks. There are also restrooms and shaded picnic tables.

Continue down the path to another bridge with a great view of the falls at 0.94 mile. (***Note:*** Some signs in the park call this waterfall "Wailele Waterfall.") There are more restrooms and a shower on the other side of the bridge. Arrive at the falls at just over a mile to find a small gear shop with water shoes, and so forth, that will store your valuables for a fee. There is also a life jacket tent with lifeguards to help you find your fit. You must wear a life jacket to swim in the pool, so grab one and jump on in! Remember to tip your friendly lifeguards and tell Johnny, Carlos, and Cruise Thompson that Justin says "Howzit."

Bring a beach towel and some sunscreen and make a fun day of it. Once you're finished chilling at the falls, make sure to leave yourself time to wander through the miles of side trails through a worldwide variety of different gardens on your way back to the car. Check out the flora and fauna of Central and South America, Fiji, Sri Lanka, Madagascar, and so many more. Watch for the peacocks and ʻalae ʻula (Hawaiian gallinule) roaming the grounds. And bask in the extensive Hawaiian history and cultural significance emanating from this place.

Waimea Falls

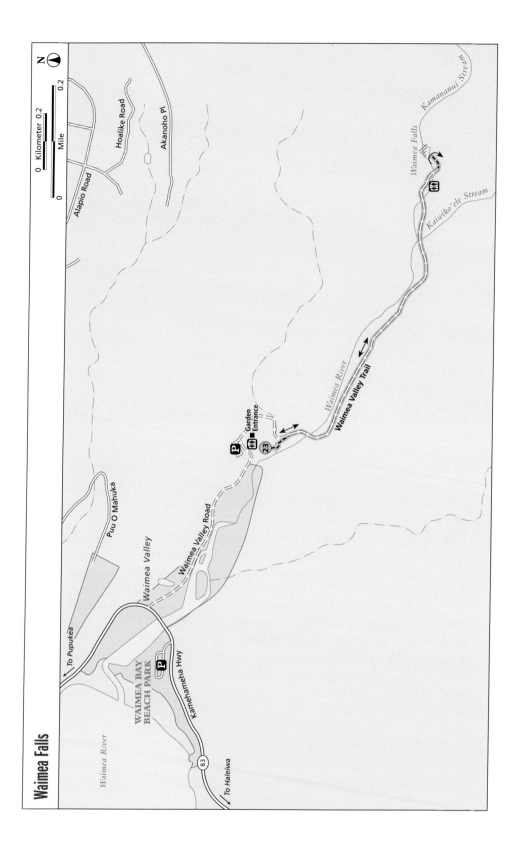

Waimea Falls

Miles and Directions

0.0 Start at the ticket office for Waimea Valley.

0.15 Cross the first bridge over the Waimea River.

0.64 The trail turns left and goes down toward the river.

0.85 Cross the second bridge over the Waimea River.

0.94 Cross the third bridge over the river with a view upstream to Waimea Falls.

1.1 The trail ends at Waimea Falls. Enjoy the falls and pool before retracing your steps.

2.2 Arrive back at the trailhead.

Additional Information

As a nonprofit botanical garden, Waimea Valley charges a fee for entry. See www .waimeavalley.net/botanical–collection for details. Swimming is free with a paid admission. Life jackets are also free with a paid admission, but remember to tip your lifeguards. There are changing rooms by the waterfall where you can change into a bathing suit and a shower beside the changing rooms.

Waimea Valley has several food and beverage concession stands open Tuesday through Sunday, including:

Hale Kope Coffee Shop, 8 a.m. to 3 p.m.

Kikoni Bar, 10 a.m. to 4:30 p.m. (open until 6 p.m. Thursday for the Hale'iwa Market)

Wahi 'Āina Grill, 10 a.m. to 4 p.m.

Wailele Snack Shop, 10 a.m. to 4 p.m.

24 La'ie Falls

From the seaside town of La'ie, home of the Polynesian Cultural Center and La'ie Hawai'i Temple, you can ascend out of the back of the valley up 3 miles of gradual, very well marked and maintained trail to a lovely set of waterfalls cascading into picturesque plunge pools. This land, and much of La'ie, is owned by the Church of Jesus Christ of Latter-day Saints, so you must obtain a permit to adventure here.

Height of falls: Multiple waterfalls between 10 and 20 feet tall

Type of falls: Tier

Start: La'ie Park

Distance: 6.2 miles out and back

Difficulty: Moderate

Hiking time: About 4 hours

Elevation change: 1,311 feet

Trail surface: Wide dirt path until the final descent to the falls, which is narrow and can be slippery

Seasons/schedule: Accessible year-round

Fees and permits: Permit required. See "Additional Information."

Land status: Private land (The Church of Jesus Christ of Latter-day Saints)

Nearest town: La'ie

Other trail users: Mountain bikers, fruit foragers, and pig hunters

Canine compatibility: Yes

Water availability: Stream water at the falls, which must be purified due to the risk of leptospirosis throughout the Hawai'i islands

Finding the trailhead: Turn off Kamehameha Highway / HI 83 onto Poohaili Street in La'ie. Park at La'ie Park on Po'ohaili Street, or at a nearby street spot, and start walking *mauka* (toward the mountains) approximately 0.6 mile to the La'ie Falls trailhead. Make sure to choose the middle road at each intersection, staying straight on Poohaili Street until you reach the blue La'ie Falls trailhead sign. Trailhead GPS: N21° 39.035', W157° 55.783'; Falls GPS: N21° 36.615', W157° 57.180'

The Hike

From the start of the trail, after your walk along 0.6 mile of flat roadbed, you will start the gradual incline toward La'ie Falls. The first 1.8 miles of trail will be mostly uncovered, providing intense sun in the middle of the day. It is partially shaded through this section with ironwood trees (which sometimes can blanket the trail with their needles) and thick strawberry guava stands (which produce a bright red fruit that is tasty), but most of it is along old service roads that have very wide sections of scarred earth, so be sure to wear sunscreen or skin-covering clothes to protect from the intense sun exposure.

At approximately 1.8 miles into the hike, you will encounter a thick grove of Cook pine trees. Their needles are noticeably thicker than the long, thin needles of the ironwoods you initially encountered on the hike. This makes for some soft spots to rest and take in the views.

Top: *A small blue sign marks the trail.*
Bottom: *The first falls you arrive at*

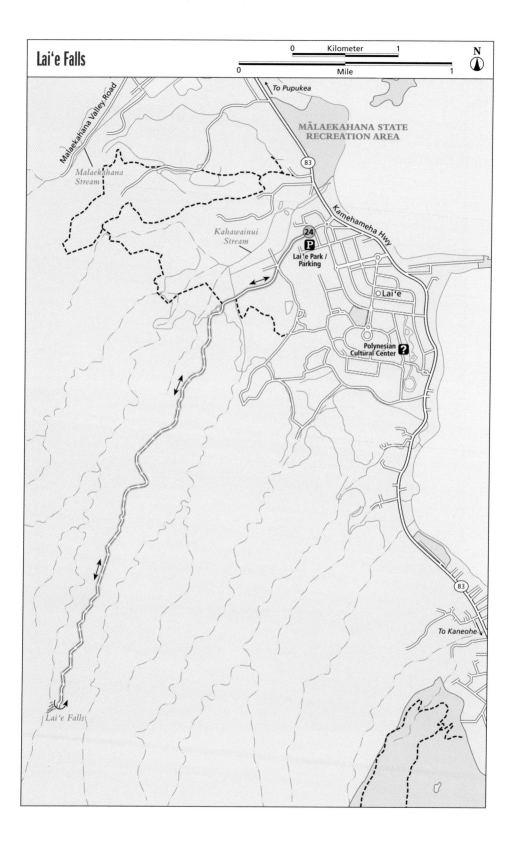

Lai'e Falls

0 Kilometer 1

0 Mile 1

N

To Pupukea

MĀLAEKAHANA STATE
RECREATION AREA

83

Malaekahana Valley Road

Malaekahana
Stream

Kamehameha Hwy

Kahawainui
Stream

24

P
Lai'e Park /
Parking

Lai'e

Polynesian
Cultural Center ?

83

To Kaneohe

Lai'e Falls

Another falls just upstream

Shortly after passing through the Cook pine forest, you will see the vegetation change again, this time to very thick strawberry guava. In the right seasons you can pick these yummy fruits for a scrumptious trail treat as you make your way up the mountain. The strawberry guava thicket is so thick that you will find it to be a tunnel in many spots. The foliage covers the trail very well, keeping the sun off of you for the rest of your journey to the falls.

At approximately 3 miles into the hike, you will come to a sign for Laʻie Falls that points you through a small cut-through in the ridgetop to a trail going down the other side of the ridge and into the valley where Laʻie Falls is located. Shortly after passing through

The trail passes through a Cook pine forest.

the cut-through, you will be able to hear the falls below. The trail becomes slightly eroded and much steeper in this final 0.1-mile section. Continue along, using ropes as necessary to balance yourself down the steep, tall steps. The small, swimmable pools and multiple waterfalls await you.

Miles and Directions

0.0 Park at Laʻie Park on Poohaili Street. Walk along the flat roadbed into the valley.

0.6 The Laʻie Falls trailhead is on your left.

1.8 Thicket of Cook pine trees.

3.0 Turn to the right and take the cut-through onto a side trail down to Laʻie Falls.

3.1 The trail ends at the many falls and pools of Laʻie Falls. Enjoy the falls before retracing your steps.

6.2 Arrive back at the trailhead.

Additional Information

Obtain a permit to hike this trail across private land from Hawaii Reserves, Inc., which manages property affiliated with the Church of Jesus Christ of Latter-day Saints. Their office is in the Laʻie Shopping Center, and they can be communicated with through www.hawaiireserves.com or by phone at (808) 293-9201. The permit is used to keep track of who is on their property, so if you don't return they will know who to look for and where.

25 Maunawili Falls

From Maunawili neighborhood you will walk 1.35 miles on a muddy trail to a cascading 25-foot-tall waterfall with a swimming pool. Watch for local cliff divers jumping off the face of the falls and both sides of the steep-walled canyon.

Note: Maunawili Falls was closed for maintenance and repairs at the time of the writing of this book. Some of the hike description may change once the trail restoration project is complete. See closure note below.

Height of falls: 25 feet
Type of falls: Plunge
Start: Intersection of Kelewina Street and Maunawili Road Park
Distance: 2.7 miles out and back
Difficulty: Moderate
Hiking time: About 2 hours (depending on how long you stay at the pool)
Elevation change: 455 feet
Trail surface: Wide muddy path with a few very slick spots and stream crossings to be careful on while traversing

Seasons/schedule: Accessible year-round. Public access for the Maunawili Trail is 6 a.m. to 6 p.m. per a trailhead sign.
Fees and permits: None
Land status: Mostly State of Hawai'i
Nearest town: Kailua
Other trail users: Pig hunters and cliff divers
Canine compatibility: Yes
Water availability: Stream water at the falls, which must be purified due to the risk of leptospirosis throughout the Hawai'i islands

Finding the trailhead: Turn off HI 61 / Pali Highway onto Auloa Road. Immediately turn left onto Maunawili Road and continue approximately 1.5 miles to the intersection of Kelewina Street and Maunawili Road, where you will find a yellow gate. Park in the neighborhood and hike past the gate. *Note:* Make sure to not slam your car doors and keep your voices low while walking through the neighborhood. Many residents leave their windows open to enjoy the cool valley breezes, so it sounds like you are in their living room when you are walking down the street by their homes. Stay very quiet until you are on the trail and well outside of the neighborhood. Trailhead GPS: N21° 21.534', W157° 45.726'; Falls GPS: N21° 20.927', W157° 46.241'

Trail closure: The entrance to Maunawili Falls from the neighborhood is closed as of July 2021. The trail restoration project is expected to last for two years, with the trail reopening in summer 2023. Please obey all posted signs and *do not trespass*. You can access Maunawili Falls from the Pali Highway or the Waimanalo entrance of the Maunawili Bigs trail. The distance from the Pali Highway to the falls is approximately 3 miles. Per the Nā Ala Hele website: "To get to the falls you will need to hike for approximately two (2) miles on the Maunawili trail until you come to Maunawili falls connector trail junction. Proceed down the trail for approximately one (1) mile to another trail junction" (https://hawaiitrails.hawaii.gov/trails/#/trail/maunawili-falls-trail -portion-of-trail-on-state-land-is-open/271, accessed 10/24/21). For more information about the alternate trailheads, see the Maunawili Bigs hike.

Falls and swimming pool

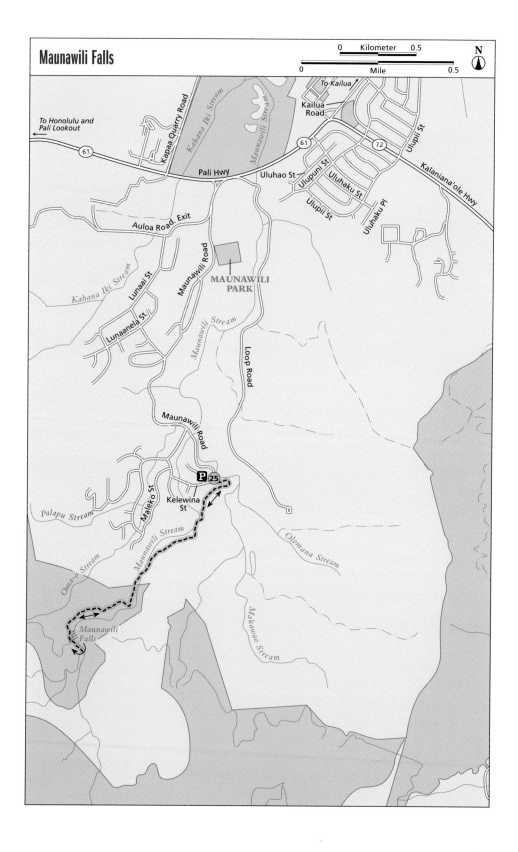

Maunawili Falls

To Kailua

Kailua
Road

To Honolulu and
Pali Lookout

61

61

72

Ulupii St

Kalaniana'ole Hwy

Kapaa Quarry Road

Kahana Iki Stream

Maunawili Stream

Pali Hwy

Uluhao St

Ulupuni St

Uluhaku St

Ulupii St

Uluhaku Pl

Auloa Road. Exit

Maunawili Road

MAUNAWILI
PARK

Kahana Iki Stream

Lunaai St

Maunawili Stream

Loop Road

Lunaanela St.

Maunawili Road

Maunawili Stream

Palapu Stream

Maleko St

Kelewina
St

P 25

Olomana Stream

Oma-o Stream

Maunawili Stream

Maunawili
Falls

Makawao Stream

The Hike

I'd suggest going in the middle of a bright, sunny day to take full advantage of the swimming pool. Start by going past the yellow gate at the intersection of Kelewina Street and Maunawili Road. Walk 330 feet down an old road (note that this road is still used by some residents, so make way for passing cars) and turn right when you see the three old green placards talking about the Agricultural Terrace Complex on your right. You will also see a beat-up sign that says "Waterfall Trail Enter Here" on the left side of the road pointing you to the right and onto the muddy, rooted trail.

Most of this hike is well covered by large shade-providing trees and vines. You will find a set of muddy stairs down the trail at 0.25 mile into your hike and a large opening in the canopy at 0.6 mile in. Look up at this opening to see the majestic Koʻolau Mountains above you.

Continue on to a stream crossing by a huge tree at 0.7 mile into your hike. Once across the stream, continue to watch your step, as you will hike across a lot of roots, many of which are full of ankle-deep mud holes between the risen roots. Continue to follow the eroded trail until you find a long set of stairs to climb up at 1.0 mile into your hike. This is another great spot to bask in the 360-degree view of the Koʻolau Mountains and Olomana peaks. Go another 0.2 mile up the trail until you come to a very long, tall bench on the right and a trail going down to your left.

Go down the steep trail, watching your step on the slick plastic boards and rocks holding the stairs together. Cross the stream at 1.27 miles into your hike and again at 1.29 miles. Once you have made these two stream crossings, you will stay in the streambed, rock-hopping your way up the stream to the falls and pool at 1.35 miles.

Miles and Directions

0.0 Start at the yellow gate at the intersection of Kelewina Street and Maunawili Road.

330 ft. Turn right off the old road onto the dirt trail.

0.7 Cross the stream beside a huge tree.

1.0 Reach a long set of stairs climbing up.

1.2 Arrive at a long, tall bench with the trail to the falls going down to the left.

1.27 Cross the stream.

1.29 Cross the stream again, then hike in the streambed to the falls.

1.35 Arrive at Maunawili Falls. Enjoy the falls and pool before retracing your steps.

2.7 Arrive back at the trailhead.

26 Maunawili Bigs

From Waikupanaha Street in Waimanalo, or from the Pali Highway just down from the Pali Lookout heading toward Kailua, you can enjoy a 10.67-mile thru-hike to massive waterfall chutes falling off of the spine of the Ko'olau Mountains.

Height of falls: Many falls, each hundreds of feet tall
Type of falls: Plunge
Start: Maunawili Ditch Trailhead on Waikupanaha Street in Waimanalo
Distance: 10.67 miles one way
Difficulty: Difficult
Hiking time: 3 to 4 hours one way (depending on how fast you go)
Elevation change: 1,855 feet

Trail surface: Narrow muddy path with a few very slick spots and stream crossings to be careful on while traversing
Seasons/schedule: Accessible year-round
Fees and permits: None
Land status: State of Hawai'i (Nā Ala Hele trails)
Nearest town: Kailua and Waimanalo
Other trail users: Pig hunters
Canine compatibility: Yes
Water availability: None. Don't count on there being water in any of the streambeds.

Finding the trailhead: At the Waimanalo end, park in the small (6 to 8 cars) parking lot at the Maunawili Ditch Trailhead on Waikupanaha Street and hike past the gate. Make sure to not slam your car doors and keep your voices low while walking through the neighborhood. Please stay quiet until you are on the trail and well outside of the neighborhood.

At the Kailua end, you will want to go north on the Pali Highway (HI 61) from Honolulu and park at the Scenic Point on your right about 1 mile past the Pali Highway tunnels in the middle of the hairpin turn just before the Saint Stephens Diocesan Center. The trail starts to your right from the lookout. Waimanalo Trailhead GPS: N21° 20.536', W157° 44.478'; Pali Highway Trailhead GPS: N21° 21.828', W157° 46.754'

The Hike

The Bigs only flow when there has been a deluge of rain for multiple days. It takes many inches of rainfall to "charge up" the hanging valleys high above Maunawili Valley. But even on a dry day, the views from this contour trail are of massive mountain cliffs reaching into the heavens and an expansive valley floor stretching to the ocean with plenty of jagged peaks sprinkled all over.

For our hike, Becca Frager and I parked the car just off the Pali Highway at the Kailua end and took a ride-share to the Waimanalo end, then jogged back. Most of this hike is along a contour, not gaining much elevation, except near Waimanalo. Going past the gate at the Maunawili Ditch Trailhead, you immediately start ascending a gradual incline. This will continue for a while, climbing around 400 feet in your first mile. Be prepared for the roller coaster of climbing out onto ridgelines and

Top: *On really wet days the Bigs become prominent waterfalls.*
Bottom: *The chutes light up after the hanging valleys have filled up.* NANDOR SZOTAK

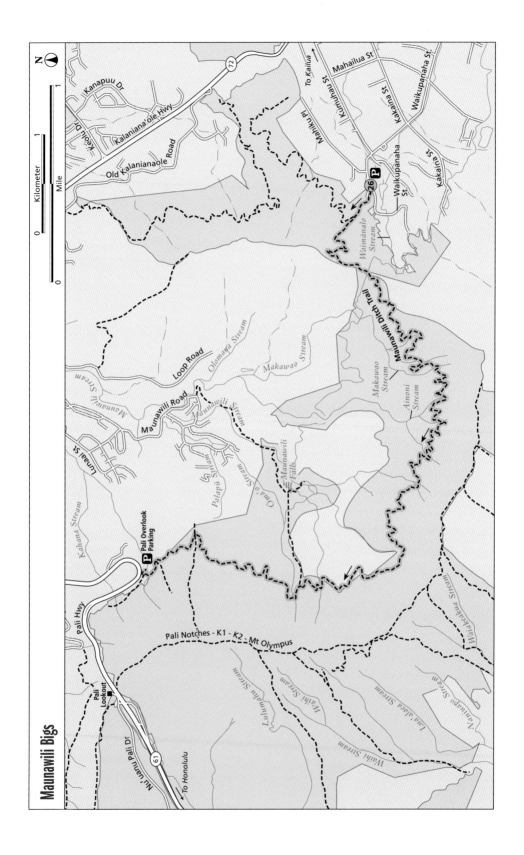

Maunawili Bigs

N

Kilometer

0   1

Mile

0   1

To Kailua

Mahailua St.

Kumuhau St.

Waikupanaha St.

Kakaina St.

Mahiku Pl.

26 P

Waikupanaha St.

Kakaina St.

72

Kanapuu Dr

Keolu Dr

Kalaniana'ole Hwy

Old Kalanianaole Road

Waumānalo Stream

Maunawili Ditch Trail

Makawao Stream

Ainoni Stream

Loop Road

Olomana Stream

Makawao Stream

Maunawili Road

Maunawili Stream

Lunaai St.

Maunawili Falls

Palapū Stream

Omo'o Stream

Kahana Stream

Maunawili Stream

Pali Overlook Parking

P

Waikakalaua Stream

Pali Hwy

Pali Notches - K1 - K2 - Mt Olympus

Pali Lookout

Nu'uanu Pali Dr

Lulumahu Stream

Waihi Stream

Palaalaea Stream

Namilimili Stream

Wahi Stream

61

To Honolulu

The closer you get, the more massive they become. NANDOR SZOTAK

dropping back down into streambeds for the next 8 miles. Then descend the last quarter-mile to your car.

You will have sweeping views of Olomana ("Three Peaks") and the Ko'olau Mountains all throughout your hike. Look up toward the Ko'olaus between miles 4.0 and 7.5 to see a variety of waterfall chutes, any one of which may flow on a wet day. When it is really wet, they flow heavily! Massive amounts of water can dump down at terminal velocity when falling up to 1,000 feet to the valley floor. Their power can feel overwhelming at times.

Make sure to be extra cautious on the slick rocks, and don't go beyond your ability. Even on a clear day you should carry your hiking essentials and be prepared for the weather to change.

Stacks of waterfalls all the way to the valley floor.
NANDOR SZOTAK

Side note: The Hawaiian Ultra Running Team (HURT) does their annual 22-mile Run with the Pigs–Maunawili Out and Back here every August.

Miles and Directions

0.0	Start at the Maunawili Ditch Trailhead in Waimanalo.
1.0	Turn left onto the Maunawili Ditch Trail (aka Maunawili Demo Trail).
4.0–7.5	Look up at the Ko'olau Mountains in search of the Maunawili Bigs.
8.4	Pass the Maunawili Falls connection.
10.5	Turn right off the Maunawili Demo Trail down toward the Scenic Point on the Pali Highway.
10.67	Arrive at the parking area for the Scenic Point on the Pali Highway.

27 Likeke Falls

Above the towns of Kailua and Kaneohe, and just below the Nu'uanu Saddle and Pali Lookout, is a family-friendly two-tiered waterfall. Park at the Ko'olau Ballrooms and Conference Center and walk 0.4 mile to a stunning cascading waterfall.

Height of falls: 20 feet
Type of falls: Tier
Start: Ko'olau Ballrooms and Conference Center parking lot
Distance: 0.8 mile out and back
Difficulty: Moderate
Hiking time: About 1 hour (depending on how long you stay at the falls)
Elevation change: 205 feet
Trail surface: Wide muddy path with a few rocky and rooty spots to be careful on

Seasons/schedule: Accessible year-round
Fees and permits: Fee to park at Ko'olau Ballrooms and Conference Center
Land status: Likely private land
Nearest town: Kailua
Other trail users: Fruit foragers
Canine compatibility: Yes
Water availability: Stream water at the falls, which must be purified due to the risk of leptospirosis throughout the Hawai'i islands

Finding the trailhead: Just off Kamehameha Highway / HI 83, turn onto Kahiko Street. Follow Kahiko Street to the end and turn right onto Kionaole Road at the T-intersection. Park outside the gates to the Ko'olau Ballrooms and Conference Center (formerly Ko'olau Golf Course) at 45-550 Kionaole Road (make sure to park with all tires off the pavement to avoid a parking ticket), or pay a fee to park inside the center and save a half mile of road walking. (Note that the parking lot is locked at 4 p.m. each day, so make sure to be out before then or park outside the gate if you think you may not make it back in time.) From the parking lot go to the upper end of the lot and find a chain gate across a single-lane paved road at the far corner away from the country club. Trailhead GPS: N21° 22.366', W157° 47.447'; Falls GPS: N21° 22.132', W157° 47.440'

The Hike

High above the towns of Kailua and Kaneohe on O'ahu's Windward Coast, you find the highest peaks in the Ko'olau Mountains and runoff flowing in every direction from them. Some of that water flows down toward the Nu'uanu Saddle and cascades into Likeke Falls below. Relatively easy when considering the conditions of Hawai'i trails, the hike to Likeke Falls is one frequented by families with small children. In just 0.4 mile you can play in the shallow stream water of a small double-tiered waterfall.

Start by crossing the chain gate in the upper back left corner of the Ko'olau Ballrooms and Conference Center parking lot. Walk up a paved single-lane road until you get to a very large graffitied water tank. Make a hard left just before the water tank and go up the muddy hill. Continue straight on the well-established trail. Pass under some power lines and enjoy the view from the opening they cut in the canopy.

Top: Park at the Koʻolau Ballrooms and Conference Center or just outside the gate.
Bottom: Quiet, clear stream

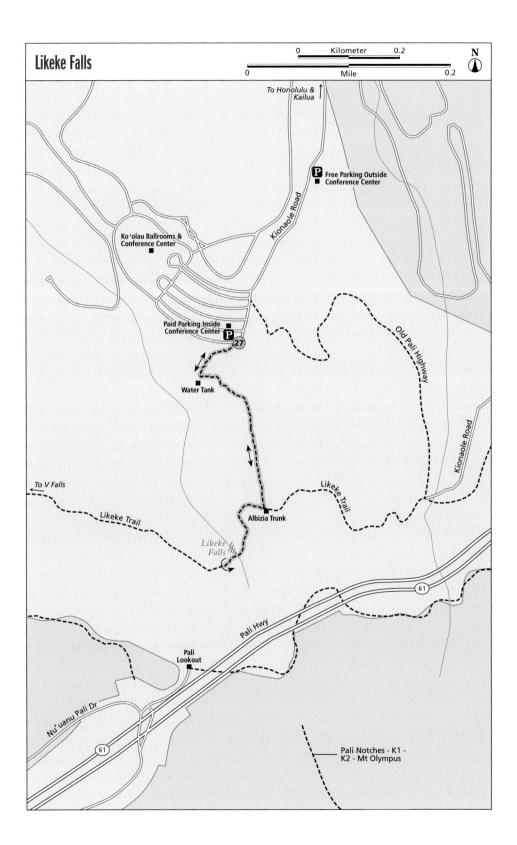

Likeke Falls

0   Kilometer   0.2

0   Mile   0.2

N

To Honolulu &
Kailua

P Free Parking Outside
Conference Center

Kionaole Road

Ko'olau Ballrooms &
Conference Center

Old Pali Highway

Paid Parking Inside
Conference Center
P
27

Kionaole Road

Water Tank

To V Falls

Likeke Trail

Likeke Trail

Albizia Trunk

Likeke
Falls

61

Pali Hwy

Pali
Lookout

Nu'uanu Pali Dr

61

Pali Notches - K1 -
K2 - Mt Olympus

So relaxing. NANDOR SZOTAK

The trail turns back and to the right and continues up a rooted, muddy trail through Albizia trees and then under a dense hau tangle. You will notice the trail soon turns to an old roadbed made of stones. Watch for the huge Albizia trunk on the right that is covered in graffiti at 0.27 mile. (At the time of this writing, there was a large blue arrow painted on the tree, but any time it is at 0.27 mile and has lots of etchings in the trunk.) Make sure to turn right here!

Walk through thick ginger, some of which remind me of corn on the cob and are called rattlesnake ginger! You will soon be back to walking under a thick hau tree tangle, which opens up to the streambed. Walk up the stream just a few more feet to see beautiful Likeke Falls at 0.4 mile. Enjoy the cascading falls and the light shooting upon them through the small opening in the canopy. Go to the opposite side of the stream from the falls and look for a muddy hill climbing up a few feet.

Even small falls can be dangerous in storms.

Step up here to see an expansive view of the valley, the windward side of O'ahu, and the ocean below you. Retrace your steps to get back to the parking lot and your car.

Miles and Directions

0.0 Hike up the trail at the back of the Ko'olau Ballrooms and Conference Center parking lot.

0.1 Turn left just before the large water tank.

0.27 Turn right off the old roadbed at the large, scratched-up Albizia tree with a spray-painted blue arrow.

0.4 Arrive at Likeke Falls. Enjoy the falls and views of the valley before retracing your steps.

0.8 Arrive back at the trailhead.

28 V Falls

Just a little further along the trail to Likeke Falls is a very tall cliff face from which flows an elegant V-shaped waterfall when there has been an extended period of very wet weather.

Height of falls: Over 200 feet
Type of falls: Plunge
Start: Koʻolau Ballrooms and Conference Center parking lot
Distance: 2.52 miles out and back
Difficulty: Difficult; requires free climbing
Hiking time: About 2.5 hours (depending on how long you stay at the pool)
Elevation change: 413 feet
Trail surface: Wide muddy path with a few rocky and rooted spots to be careful on

Seasons/schedule: Accessible year-round
Fees and permits: Fee to park at Koʻolau Ballrooms and Conference Center
Land status: Likely private land
Nearest town: Kailua
Other trail users: Fruit foragers
Canine compatibility: Yes
Water availability: Stream water at the falls, which must be purified due to the risk of leptospirosis throughout the Hawaiʻi islands

Finding the trailhead: Just off Kamehameha Highway / HI 83, turn onto Kahiko Street. Follow Kahiko Street to the end and turn right onto Kionaole Road at the T-intersection. Park outside the gates to the Koʻolau Ballrooms and Conference Center (formerly Koʻolau Golf Course) at 45-550 Kionaole Road (make sure to park with all tires off the pavement to avoid a parking ticket), or pay a fee to park inside the conference center and save a half mile of road walking. (Note that the parking lot is locked at 4 p.m. each day, so make sure to be out before then or park outside the gate if you think you may not make it back in time.) From the parking lot go to the upper end of the lot and find a chain gate across a single-lane paved road at the far corner away from the country club. Trailhead GPS: N21° 22.366', W157° 47.447'; Falls GPS: N21° 22.293', W157° 48.109'

The Hike

Pass Likeke Falls and continue down the "trail" on the far side to the left as you are looking out from the falls. You will realize why I put quotation marks around *trail* very quickly, as you are soon tromping through a flowing stream and deep puddles of mud. Watch your head on the low-hanging hau tangles and your steps as you climb up and down through the ends of many small gulches.

See more rattlesnake ginger and then enjoy the vibrant red blooms of shampoo ginger at 0.57 mile. Say a wish for fruiting mountain apple trees at 0.62 mile. You then walk through yellow strawberry guava, which opens up to two monster mango trees in a grassy meadow at 0.66 mile. This trail has it all!

Stay left as you cross a small stream at 0.88 mile. There is a large clearing with dramatic views all the way to Kaneohe Bay at 0.96 mile. You then pass an even more massive mango tree in a small grassy meadow at 1.03 miles.

Above: Is it corn? Or ginger?
Below: Make sure to look up from time to time.

V Falls

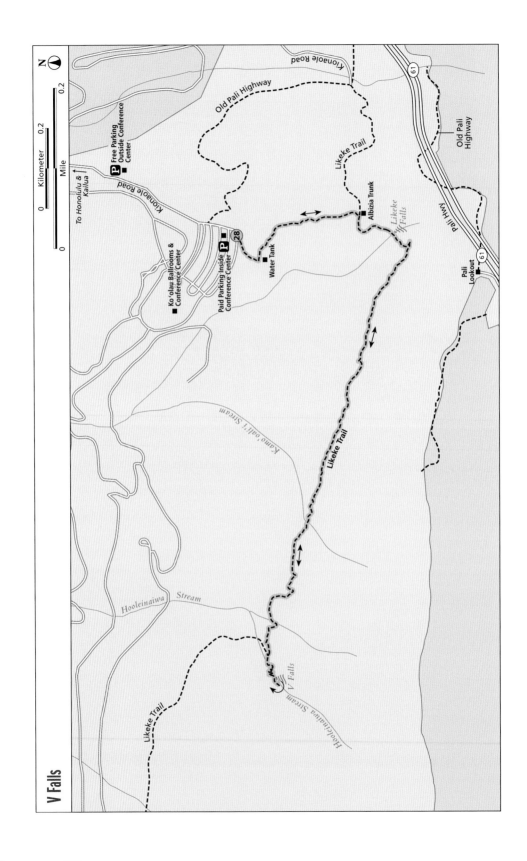

N

Kilometer
0   0.2
Mile
0   0.2

To Honolulu &
Kailua

Free Parking
Outside Conference
Center

Kionaole Road

Ko'olau Ballrooms &
Conference Center

Paid Parking Inside
Conference Center

28

Water Tank

Old Pali Highway

Kionaole Road

Albizia Trunk

Likeke Trail

Likeke
Falls

Kamo'oali'i Stream

Likeke Trail

Hooleinaiwa   Stream

Likeke Trail

V Falls

Hooleinaiwa Stream

Pali Hwy

Pali
Lookout

61

Old Pali
Highway

61

It may not look like much . . .

Continue on the trail until 1.26 miles, when you come to a switchback with a side trail going straight up into the gulch. Turn up this stream and climb your way into the overgrown gulch until you reach the headwall at 1.4 miles.

Enjoy V Falls responsibly! *Do not go if the weather is too wet!* If the water is brown at Likeke Falls, turn around, don't drown! Try to time it on the heels of a wet few days, after the storms have passed but while the mountains are still flowing lots of water out of their high-hanging pools.

Miles and Directions

0.0 Hike up the trail at the back of the Ko'olau Ballrooms and Conference Center parking lot.

0.1 Turn left just before the large water tank.

Sometimes it really flows! NANDOR SZOTAK

0.27 Turn right off the old roadbed at the large scratched-up Albizia tree with a spray-painted blue arrow.

0.4 Pass Likeke Falls, continuing down the "trail."

0.66 Pass a large meadow with two big mango trees.

0.88 Stay left after crossing a small stream.

1.26 Turn left onto a side trail going up into the gulch to arrive at V Falls. Enjoy the falls before retracing your steps.

2.52 Arrive back at the trailhead.

29 Waipuilani Falls

Experience another massive waterfall by hiking to the base of the monster you see on your right while driving across the Pali Highway from town (Honolulu) to Kailua.

Height of falls: 420 feet
Type of falls: Plunge
Start: Across from the Kailua-bound exit ramp when leaving the Pali Lookout
Distance: 2.08 miles out and back
Difficulty: Moderate
Hiking time: 1.5 to 2 hours (depending on how long you stay at the falls)
Elevation change: 283 feet
Trail surface: Rugged and rooted dirt path with a few muddy climbs to be careful on while traversing

Seasons/schedule: Accessible year-round. The parking lot for the Pali Lookout closes each evening, so make sure to park outside the gate or be out prior to the lot closing.
Fees and permits: None
Land status: Round Top Forest Reserve
Nearest town: Either Honolulu or Kailua; you're about halfway between the two.
Other trail users: None
Canine compatibility: Yes
Water availability: Stream water at the falls, which must be purified due to the risk of leptospirosis throughout the Hawai'i islands

Finding the trailhead: Take the exit off the Pali Highway / HI 61 like you were going to the Nu'uanu Pali Lookout when heading from Honolulu toward Kailua. Slow down, the trailhead is just a couple hundred feet up on your right. The obscure trailhead is directly across from the Kailua-bound exit ramp back onto the Pali Highway if you were driving down from the overlook and continuing on to Kailua. Park just off the road where the two exit ramps diverge. The trail starts into the woods here. Trailhead GPS: N21° 21.843', W157° 47.671'; Falls GPS: N21° 21.342', W157° 47.682'

The Hike

Watch for the obscure trailhead along the Kailua-bound side of the exit off the Pali Highway at the Pali Lookout—it is directly across from the steep exit back onto the highway if you were to continue Kailua-bound. You will almost immediately cross through a large storm-drain concrete ditch. Once you climb out of the ditch you will stay to the right, then hike up some switchbacks and into a pine forest.

Stay left off the ridgetop at 0.16 mile and enter a deep streambed at 0.2 mile. Take the trail across the streambed and slightly (10 to 20 feet) to the left. The entrance to this trail looks small, but there are steps out the back. Follow this trail out of the streambed and turn right at 0.22 mile.

Go past some bright orange paperbark eucalyptus trees. The ground cover gradually changes from strawberry guava to bamboo. The trail goes steeply downhill at 0.44 mile, and you will cross another streambed at 0.52 mile.

Rock-hop the last bit to the falls.

Turn left at 0.57 mile into a thick forest of Cook pine trees, then turn left again at 0.65 mile into another grove of paperbark eucalyptus. Look for blue paint on the tree at the intersection (and along much of the trail to Waipuilani Falls). Continue up the trail behind the blue paint.

You will turn left again when you get to the stream at 0.8 mile. Follow the stream uphill to find a cute waterfall on your right at 0.93 mile. The trail then climbs away from the stream a bit, but soon pops out of the canopy at Waipuilani Falls at 1.04 miles into your hike.

Two falls and a cave!

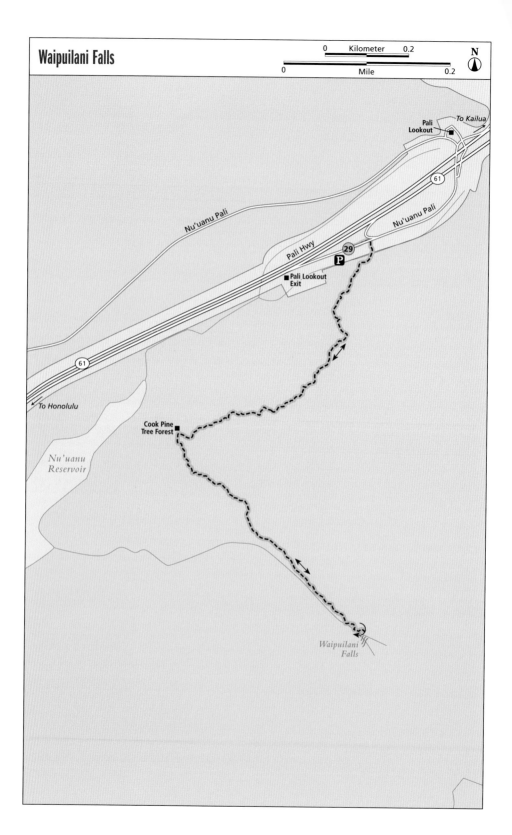

Waipuilani Falls

0   Kilometer   0.2
0   Mile   0.2

N

To Kailua

Pali Lookout

61

Nu'uanu Pali

Nu'uanu Pali

Pali Hwy

29

P

Pali Lookout Exit

61

To Honolulu

Cook Pine Tree Forest

Nu'uanu Reservoir

Waipuilani Falls

Waipuilani is the falls on the right. NANDOR SZOTAK

Enjoy all 440 feet of beautiful cascading falls. By studying the massive wall you will realize there are actually two canyons dumping their streams into two waterfalls flowing down the rock face. In between the two falls you will see a small cave in the middle about 10 feet from the bottom of the falls. This is an ancient cave, likely dug by the sugarcane plantations to secure water during times of drought. Enjoy the falls but beware of rockfalls, never fully letting your guard down.

Miles and Directions

0.0 Start at the Kailua-bound exit ramp to the Pali Lookout by entering the forest at the obscure trailhead.

0.2 Go through a deep streambed, climbing back out on the trail across the stream and slightly to the left.

0.52 Cross another streambed.

0.57 Turn left into a thick forest of Cook pine trees.

0.65 Turn left into more paperbark eucalyptus trees (look for blue paint on the tree at the intersection).

0.8 The trail meets the stream and continues up it.

0.93 A small waterfall is on your right.

1.04 The trail ends at Waipuilani Falls. Enjoy the view before retracing your steps.

2.08 Arrive back at the trailhead.

30 Lulumahu Falls

From the side of the Pali Highway, you can walk a short 0.9 mile of rugged trail to a 350-foot waterfall high up Lulumahu Stream. You will walk through a dense bamboo forest, across an ancient sugarcane dam, along a sugarcane irrigation ditch, and up a streambed of slick rocks to a spectacular multiple-tiered waterfall.

Height of falls: Approximately 350 feet total; lowest tier is approximately 100 feet tall.

Type of falls: Tier

Start: Dirt parking lot where the Pali Highway meets Nu'uanu Road

Distance: 1.8 miles out and back

Difficulty: Intermediate due to deep mud, slick rocks, and stream crossings. Lightweight and quick-to-dry hiking or water shoes suggested.

Hiking time: About 2 hours (depending on how long you stay at the pool)

Elevation change: 339 feet

Trail surface: Worn, muddy path with many slick and/or rocky spots to be careful on while traversing

Seasons/schedule: Accessible year-round. The parking lot has experienced lots of break-ins; and the bamboo forest is difficult to navigate in the dark, so make sure to be out prior to sunset.

Fees and permits: Permit required. Obtain a free permit from the Hawai'i Department of Land and Natural Resources, https://trails .ehawaii.gov/camping/welcome.html.

Land status: Round Top Forest Reserve; restricted watershed

Nearest town: Honolulu

Other trail users: Pig hunters and Hawai'i preservationists

Canine compatibility: Yes

Water availability: Stream water at the falls, which must be purified due to the risk of lepto-spirosis throughout the Hawai'i islands

Finding the trailhead: Park at the large dirt parking lot where the Pali Highway / HI 61 meets Nu'uanu Road and look for the large blue sign saying "Nu'uanu Public Hunting Area Unit E" along the chain-link fence line. As you are driving the Pali Highway from town (Honolulu), the road will be three lanes. The parking lot is on your right just before the road narrows from three lanes down to two lanes. If you continue on and find that you are on a section of highway where there are only two lanes heading toward Kailua, you have gone too far. You can turn around at the Pali Lookout and come back. *Caution:* Car break-ins are common at the trailhead parking lot. Leave your valuables in your residence or take them with you. Leave nothing in sight in the cabin of your vehicle. Trailhead GPS: N21° 21.220', W157° 48.570'; Falls GPS: N21° 20.889', W157° 48.046'

The Hike

Get ready to get muddy! And wet! And overwhelmed by the beauty of this sacred place. Makai Nu'uanu Valley is where all of Honolulu's downtown sits, including the capitol and Iolani Palace (the only foreign palace on American soil). Head inland and you find foreign embassies, exclusive clubs, and jaw-dropping views of sheer cliffs as you make your way to the summit of the Ko'olau Mountains. Cool trade winds shoot up and over the Koʻolaus, through the Nuʻuanu Saddle, and down toward downtown Honolulu and Honolulu Harbor. Years ago, King Kamehameha III spent his summers in the upper parts of Nuʻuanu Valley, near Lulumahu, most likely to beat the summer heat in Honolulu.

Start from the opening in the fence below the big blue sign reading "Nuʻuanu Public Hunting Area Unit E" out the back of the dirt parking lot on the side of the Pali Highway (prone to car break-ins). You will immediately find yourself in a thick bamboo forest. You will walk straight and slightly to your right, traveling a few hundred feet to a gravel and dirt roadbed.

Turn left on the gravel roadbed, toward the mountains. Go through lots more bamboo and fragrant ginger. Turn left again at 0.2 mile and you will soon go across a small concrete dam with a cutout in the middle that you must step across while the water flows below you.

Look for this sign to start.

Go straight through the deep dirt ditch at 0.4 mile. Turn right toward the mountains at 0.5 mile.

Walk along the old road beside an irrigation ditch to a picturesque stone dam with cascading falls glowing across it at 0.57 mile. This is not Lulumahu Falls, just an added bonus! Watch your step across the dam, as it can get slick. It is usually wiser just to go for it and walk through the wet streambed. You will most certainly wind up with wet feet by the end of the hike anyway. Might as well embrace it and enjoy it!

Stay on the trail to the left side of the stream, keeping the stream in earshot the entire time. Cross the stream at 0.67 mile. Stay near/along the stream—*do not* follow trails leading up the steep hillsides.

There are a few more stream crossings at 0.8 mile before you quickly find the massive Lulumahu Falls at 0.9 mile. Beware of falling rocks, but enjoy the amazing height of these constantly flowing falls. Coming off the two tallest mountains in the Koʻolau Mountains—Konahuanui I and Konahuanui II—this water seems to come straight from the heavens. Alas, it does not. *Do not* drink the water without first purifying it. A variety of water purifiers are available in town at Uloha–Hawaiʻi's Hiking Store.

Watch your step.

Look closely and you can observe a small cave in the lower left face of the falls, a Buddha statue with offerings, multiple tiers of falls stretching as far as the eye can see, and so much more. Make sure to head back well in advance of the dark, as the trail through the bamboo gets very spooky and hard to follow in the fading light. Remember, you are only halfway through your hike when you arrive at the water-fall. Make sure to check sunset time and have a turn-around time if you leave in the afternoon.

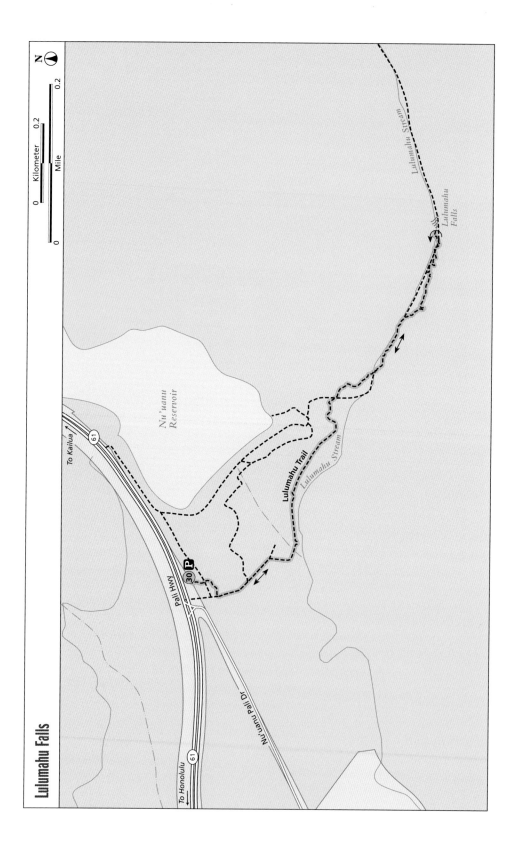

Lulumahu Falls

Multiple tiers of falls

Such a pretty veil

Miles and Directions

0.0 Start at the dirt parking lot where the Pali Highway meets Nu'uanu Road and hike through the fence at the blue sign reading "Nu'uanu Public Hunting Area Unit E."

0.1 Stay slightly right and follow the trail to a gravel road, then turn left on the road.

0.2 Turn left and go across a concrete dam.

0.4 The trail goes straight through a deep ditch.

0.5 The trail turns right toward the mountains.

0.57 Arrive at an old stone dam, traversing upstream and back to the trail on the left side of the stream.

0.67 Cross the stream, now hiking up the trail on the right side of the streambed.

0.8 Cross the stream a few more times.

0.9 The trail ends at Lulumahu Falls. Enjoy the view before retracing your steps.

1.8 Arrive back at the trailhead.

31 Jackass Ginger Pool and Falls

Just a little up the Pali from Honolulu, you turn onto the Old Pali Road and find the Judd Trail trailhead. Walk past major motion-picture sites and a section of the HURT 100 trail-running bliss to a great pool for swimming.

Height of falls: 10 feet
Type of falls: Fan
Start: Judd Trail trailhead
Distance: 0.52 mile out and back
Difficulty: Moderate
Hiking time: About 1.5 hours (depending on how long you stay at the pool)
Elevation change: 130 feet
Trail surface: Wide muddy path with a few rocky and rooty spots to be careful on while traversing

Seasons/schedule: Accessible year-round
Fees and permits: None
Land status: Honolulu watershed
Nearest town: Honolulu
Other trail users: Fruit foragers, families, dog walkers, and trail runners
Canine compatibility: Yes
Water availability: Stream water at the falls, which must be purified due to the risk of leptospirosis throughout the Hawai'i islands

Finding the trailhead: From Honolulu, take the Pali Highway / HI 61 toward Kailua 1.3 miles and turn right onto Nu'uanu Pali Drive. Take Nu'uanu Pali Drive 1 mile and look for the small road-side parking area (2 or 3 cars) on your right with large concrete pillars lying beside the road. You will see the Judd Trail sign. If this small lot is full (and it often is), just drive a bit farther and park somewhere along Nu'uanu Pali Drive. Make sure all tires are off the road when you park to avoid a ticket. Take your valuables with you. Trailhead GPS: N21° 20.804', W157° 49.166'; Falls GPS: N21° 20.787', W157° 49.270'

The Hike

Here's another great waterfall on Nu'uanu Stream. Just a short drive out of downtown Honolulu, Jackass Ginger is a local favorite. Crowds gather here to beat the summer heat and watch the daredevil divers. The rocks are taller than the water is deep, so diving here is for professionals only. Luckily there is a good pool to soak in and even a few solo soaking spots on the wall of the falls. Like an ice bath in the middle of July, this is a great spot to relax and restore in the middle of an adventurous week or a long trail run.

Start from the Judd Trail trailhead and rock-hop or ford straight across Nu'uanu Stream. Turn right immediately after the stream and follow it down a very muddy, washed out, and unmaintained trail. You will walk through a bamboo forest as the trail stays close to the stream. At approximately 0.16 mile you will see the trail climbing to the left up some muddy roots. Follow the trail up and away from the stream and out of the bamboo.

Top: Start on the Judd Trail.
Bottom: As seen in Kong: Skull Island

Stay on the right side of the trail until 0.23 mile into your hike where the trail turns back down toward the stream. Watch for a hidden double-arrow trail sign. Turn downhill, taking the makeshift trail down cut-out steps in the mud and tree roots. Choose your steps wisely as you walk down a muddy, slick set of ad hoc stairs to the

Top: The trail turns back down to the stream.
Bottom: An oasis on a hot summer day

waterfall and pool. Play in the pool and 10-foot-tall falls, but do not walk up the mowed yards at the back of the streamside homes.

I sat here once and watched a bluish-colored centipede go from being stuck on a stick in the middle of the river to climbing under the water and along the tree limb

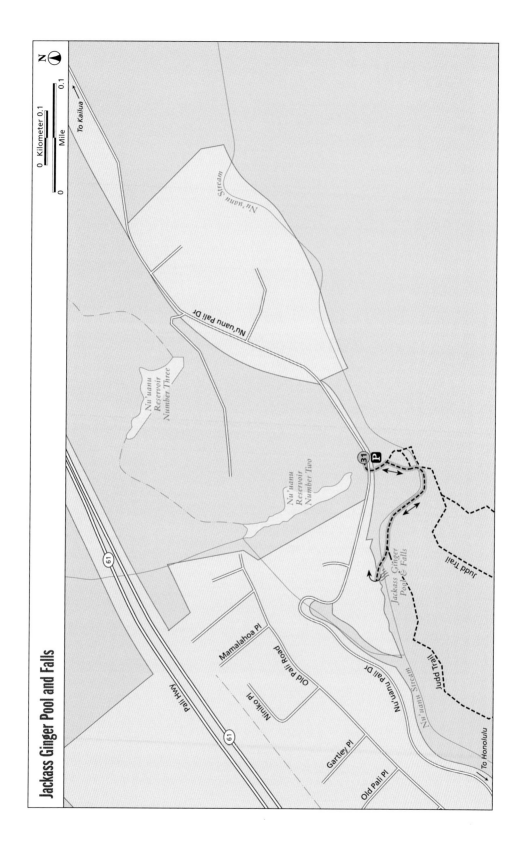

Jackass Ginger Pool and Falls

Pali Hwy

61

Mamalahoa Pl

Niniko Pl

Old Pali Road

Gartley Pl

Old Pali Pl

Nu'uanu Pali Dr

Nu'uanu Stream

Judd Trail

Judd Trail

Jackass Ginger Pool & Falls

31

P

Nu'uanu Reservoir Number Two

Nu'uanu Reservoir Number Three

Nu'uanu Pali Dr

Nu'uanu Stream

To Kailua

To Honolulu

N

0   Kilometer   0.1

0   Mile   0.1

Small falls, big pool

and out of sight. I was haunted for days at the thought of centipedes being able to swim or go fully submerged underwater. I have also sat in one of the tiny pools on the wall of this waterfall and used it as an ice bath after a long run. The HURT 100 goes along the Judd Trail, passing Jackass Ginger ten times in 100 miles of trail running. I must say it gets more and more tempting to jump in with each loop of the race!

Bring a beach towel or hammock and hang out a bit under the shaded stream-side while cheering on those brave enough to take the leap. Pack out what you pack in, and maybe even bring a garbage bag to collect waste that flows down Nuʻuanu Stream on your way out. Let's work together to leave these amazing spots as good as or better than we found them.

Miles and Directions

0.0 Start on the Judd Trail, hiking straight in.

0.05 Turn right immediately after rock-hopping across Nuʻuanu Stream.

0.16 The trail turns up out of the streambed.

0.23 The trail turns down to the right and climbs back down to the stream at a sign pointing both left and right.

0.26 The trail ends at Jackass Ginger falls and pool. Enjoy the falls before retracing your steps.

0.52 Arrive back at the trailhead.

32 Luakaha Falls

Another great falls along Nuʻuanu Stream is hidden off Nuʻuanu Pali Drive between Lulumahu Falls and the Judd Trail / Jackass Ginger pool and falls. Be ready to watch the trail carefully and follow it down a steep grade if you want to see more than just the top of the falls.

Height of falls: 50 feet
Type of falls: Horsetail
Start: Trailhead off Nuʻuanu Pali Drive just east of Nuʻuanu Reservoir 3
Distance: 0.6 mile out and back
Difficulty: Moderate
Hiking time: About 1 hour (depending on how long you stay at the pool)
Elevation change: 100 feet
Trail surface: Wide dirt path with a few slick, muddy, and rocky spots to be careful on while traversing
Seasons/schedule: Accessible year-round

Fees and permits: Permit required. Obtain a free permit from the Hawaiʻi Department of Land and Natural Resources at https://trails .ehawaii.gov/camping/welcome.html.
Land status: Restricted watershed. Round Top Forest Reserve while on the trail, but the mowed yard across from the waterfall is private land.
Nearest town: Honolulu
Other trail users: Those who own the land around Luakaha and cultural preservationists
Canine compatibility: No
Water availability: Stream water at the stream, which must be purified due to the risk of lepto-spirosis throughout the Hawaiʻi islands

Finding the trailhead: From Honolulu, take the Pali Highway / HI 61 toward Kailua 1.3 miles and turn right onto Nuʻuanu Pali Drive. Take Nuʻuanu Pali Drive 1.3 miles and look for the small roadside parking area (1 or 2 cars) on your left with an open field, Nuʻuanu Reservoir 3, and a water pumping station. If this small lot is full (and it often is), just drive a bit farther and park somewhere along Nuʻuanu Pali Drive. Make sure all tires are off the road when you park to avoid a ticket or tow. Take your valuables with you, and please be courteous to the local residents. The trailhead is obscure and slightly hidden by the very dense jungle foliage and bamboo, but you will see a small brown sign with yellow lettering that reads "Restricted Watershed—Entry by Permit Only—Commercial Activity Is Prohibited." Trailhead GPS: N21° 21.047', W157° 48.929'; Falls GPS: N21° 20.942', W157° 48.814'

The Hike

Once you find the obscure trailhead, stay straight through the bamboo. You will quickly find yourself on a wide and flat trail that is an old roadbed. This trail will take you through dense tropical rainforest. You will see a sign on your right explaining that you are entering a restricted watershed regulated by the Department of Land and Natural Resources. It explains that there are ancient Hawaiian ruins and relics in this area that must be preserved for Hawaiʻi's future. And again, entry is by permit only, so make sure to get a permit before entering this area.

Above: Do not disturb the ruins.
Below: Stay left at the ditch.

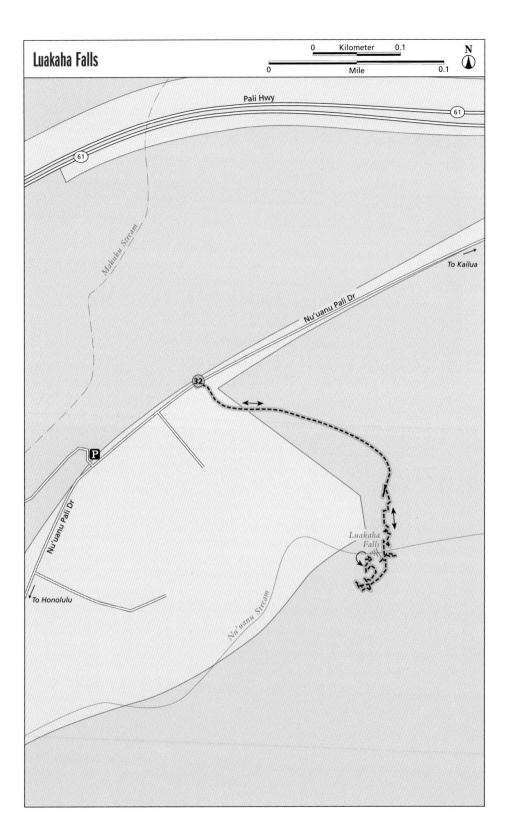

Luakaha Falls

0   Kilometer   0.1

0   Mile   0.1

N

Pali Hwy

61

61

Makuku Stream

To Kailua

Nuʻuanu Pali Dr

32

P

Nuʻuanu Pali Dr

To Honolulu

Luakaha Falls

Nuʻuanu Stream

Wide, flowing veil

Top: Look upstream to find an upper falls.
Bottom: Even an upper pool!

Continue straight on the trail and watch for a concrete irrigation ditch/canal at 0.18 mile into your hike. Stay to the left of the ditch! If you find yourself tromping through mud under a very large banyan tree, you have likely missed the left turn. When I visited, there was a lot of bamboo almost hiding the trail, so just remember that when you find the concrete ditch, you know you need to stay to the left of it.

Heavy flow

You will soon cross a large metal pipe and follow the ditch until 0.22 mile into your hike, where the trail crosses the irrigation ditch and turns down to your right. Follow a tree-rooted path to the stream and falls. There is a nice, small falls with a pool above the main falls. Enjoy the strawberry guava and ginger blooms as you make your way along the rough trail to the top of Luakaha Falls.

The top of the falls is the end of the trail. Use extreme caution near the top. I advise you to take in the view, and then turn around here.

There is a super-slick and steep down-climb to the base of the falls if you cross over to the far side of the stream and climb the muddy trail up. *Do not climb* down the rock face, as there are remnants of an old trail you can follow if you stay on the muddy trail and look for it to eventually turn to the right and go down a valley to the base of the falls. *Do not enter* the mowed yard at the base of the falls, as it is someone's private backyard!

Pack out what you pack in, and maybe even bring a garbage bag to collect waste that flows down Nu'uanu Stream on your way out. Let's always leave these amazing spots as good or better than we found them.

Miles and Directions

0.0   Start at the obscure trail off Nu'uanu Pali Road just east of Nu'uanu Reservoir 3, going straight into the dense bamboo.

0.18 Stay to the left of the irrigation ditch.

0.22 The trail turns down to the right, leaving the irrigation ditch.

0.3   The trail ends at the top of Luakaha Falls. Enjoy the views and small falls upstream before retracing your steps.

0.6   Arrive back at the trailhead.

33 Kapena Falls

From the heart of Honolulu (locally referred to as "town"), you can walk a short 0.16 mile of flat, very well marked and maintained trail to a lovely waterfall cascading into the very large Alapena Pool. You will encounter ancient petroglyphs and many cascading waterfalls along your path to a great pool for swimming.

Height of falls: 15 feet
Type of falls: Fan
Start: Nuʻuanu Memorial Park and Mortuary
Distance: 0.32 mile out and back
Difficulty: Easy
Hiking time: About 30 minutes (depending on how long you stay at the pool)
Elevation change: 20 feet
Trail surface: Wide dirt path with a few rocky spots to be careful on while traversing
Seasons/schedule: Accessible year-round. The parking lot for the cemetery closes at 4:30 p.m., so make sure to be out prior to that.

Fees and permits: None, but say hi to maintenance workers Greg and Roque at the trailhead.
Land status: Likely private
Nearest town: Honolulu
Other trail users: Homeless residents of the valley, fruit foragers, and cliff divers
Canine compatibility: Yes
Water availability: Stream water at the falls, which must be purified due to the risk of leptospirosis throughout the Hawaiʻi islands

Finding the trailhead: Take Nuʻuanu Avenue 1.7 miles up from downtown Honolulu and turn right into Nuʻuanu Memorial Park and Mortuary. Drive to the end of the road down to the left. Park in the large parking lot near the maintenance shed at the back of the memorial park on Nuʻuanu Avenue, or at a nearby street spot, and start walking the trail to the right side of the maintenance shed at the bottom of the parking lot. Stay very quiet until you are on the trail and make sure to be respectful of those paying respects to their lost loved ones, especially if there is a funeral in progress when you arrive. Trailhead GPS: N21° 19.428', W157° 50.728'; Falls GPS: N21° 19.507', W157° 50.674'

The Hike

I'd suggest a bright, sunny day to experience the full grandeur of this place. Start from the left side of the maintenance barn at the bottom of the parking lot in the back of the cemetery. You will immediately notice large, exposed boulders on the left side of the trail. You will walk beside massive banyan trees and their sprawling root systems all around the babbling stream you are on the bank of as you easily ascend a very low uphill grade.

If you look closely you will even observe ancient Hawaiian petroglyphs! Take some time to look away from the stream and to your left early in your hike to see the many petroglyphs, some of which are protected behind wrought-iron enclosures. Do not tamper with these historic ruins!

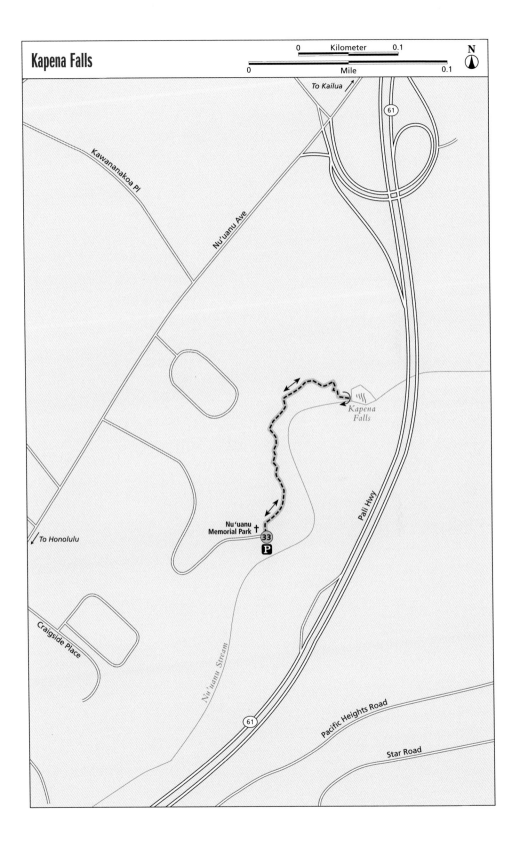

Kapena Falls

To Kailua

61

Kawananakoa Pl

Nu'uanu Ave

Kapena Falls

Pali Hwy

To Honolulu

Nu'uanu
Memorial Park

33

P

Nu'uanu Stream

Craigside Place

61

Pacific Heights Road

Star Road

N

0   Kilometer   0.1

0   Mile   0.1

A large cliff overshadows the falls.

Kapu *means "sacred"—please respect this place.*

Continue upstream, taking in the various small falls and cascades to your right. Approximately 0.16 mile ahead you will find a very large pool fed by a beautiful 15-foot waterfall. The pool is deep and there is an island in the middle of the stream. It's almost impossible not to rock-hop across the creek to the center island and then on across to the other side where there is a trail climbing up to a 35-foot rock outcropping that experienced cliff divers use to practice for their more intense ocean heroics.

Pack or wear your water shoes up this short gem of a trail in the city and quickly find yourself floating lazily or jumping wildly in an ice-cold mountain bath. Bring a beach towel or hammock and hang out a bit while cheering on those brave enough to take the leap. Pack out what you pack in, and maybe even bring a garbage bag to collect waste that flows down Nu'uanu Stream on your way out. Let's always leave these amazing spots as good or better than we found them.

Miles and Directions

0.0 Hike up the trail to the left of the maintenance shed for Nu'uanu Memorial Park and Mortuary.

0.16 Arrive at Kapena Falls. Enjoy the falls and large pool before retracing your steps.

0.32 Arrive back at the trailhead.

34 Makiki Valley Falls

Hike into a dense tropical rainforest and to a hidden waterfall just minutes from downtown Honolulu and Waikiki.

Height of falls: 35 feet
Type of falls: Plunge
Start: Hawai'i Nature Center parking lot
Distance: 2.62 miles out and back
Difficulty: Difficult due to climbing off the trail and up to the waterfall
Hiking time: 1 to 1.5 hours (depending on how long you stay at the falls)
Elevation change: 500 feet
Trail surface: Wide dirt path up Kanealole, then a narrow muddy path with rocky spots to be careful on while traversing

Seasons/schedule: Accessible year-round
Fees and permits: None
Land status: Round Top Forest Reserve
Nearest town: Honolulu
Other trail users: Fruit foragers and pig hunters
Canine compatibility: Yes
Water availability: Water fountain, water hose, and restrooms at Hawai'i Nature Center

Finding the trailhead: Turn off Nehoa Street onto Makiki Street, then immediately turn left onto Makiki Heights Drive. Continue 0.4 mile and turn right into the parking lot for the Hawai'i Nature Center. Park in the large gravel parking lot on your left just before the gate, then hike up the pedestrian path to the left of the gate. Follow the hiking trail signs until you arrive at the Hawai'i Nature Center in approximately a quarter mile. The trail crosses the road and goes to the back of the Nature Center. You will pass restrooms on your left and then go across a green bridge to the trailhead signs. Trailhead GPS: N21° 18.841', W157° 49.676'; Falls GPS: N21° 19.523', W157° 49.249'

The Hike

After hiking 0.27 mile up the pedestrian trail from the parking lot, you arrive at some covered picnic tables, a water fountain, and restrooms. Go across the bridge after passing the restrooms to arrive at several Nā Ala Hele brown signs with yellow lettering below a colorful Tantalus Trailway map by Tony Barnhill. Follow the wide gravel and dirt path to the left, going up the Kanealole Trail. Continue along the stream and follow the stairs to the right past a *loi* terrace.

Turn left at the fork at 0.38 mile to stay on the Kanealole Trail. Cross two bridges and through a forest of native Hawaiian plants. Although it is a state-maintained trail, there will be muddy and narrow sections with slick roots and rocks. Watch out for the slick water pipes protruding from the trail as you ascend. They have some sharp edges and jagged bolts sticking out toward the trail in spots, so please use caution around the pipes.

Turn down onto an obscure trail to your right at 1.1 miles. You will hear the water flowing over an old concrete dam. Climb down to the dam on the slick, muddy trail.

Free-falling waters

Makiki Valley Falls

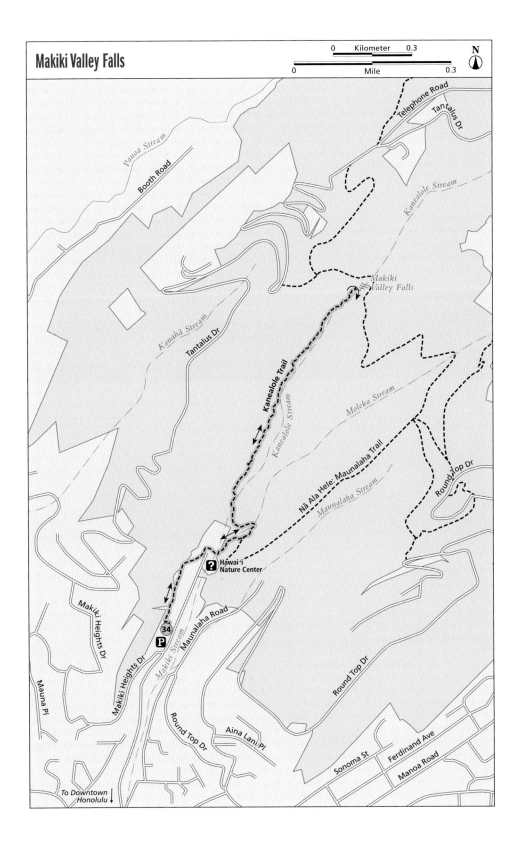

0 — Kilometer — 0.3

0 — Mile — 0.3

N

Yauoa Stream

Booth Road

Telephone Road

Tantalus Dr

Kanealole Stream

Makiki Valley Falls

Kanahā Stream

Tantalus Dr

Kanealole Trail

Kanealole Stream

Moleka Stream

Nā Ala Hele: Maunalaha Trail

Maunalaha Stream

Round Top Dr

Hawai'i Nature Center

?

Maunalaha Road

34

P

Makiki Heights Dr

Makiki Heights Dr

Makiki Stream

Mauna Pl

Round Top Dr

Aina Lani Pl

Round Top Dr

Sonoma St

Ferdinand Ave

Manoa Road

To Downtown Honolulu ↓

Irrigation tunnel near the falls

Just across the bridge from the Hawai'i Nature Center

Walk across the top of the dam to the far side of the creek, and follow this unmaintained trail upstream through deep mud and low branches. You will see an old irrigation tunnel on your right at 1.2 miles. Climb up the last section of slick rocks to a free-falling waterfall at 1.31 miles.

Tony Barnhill of the Tantalus Historical Society researched the falls and much of Makiki Valley at the Bishop Museum. He found old photos by W. E. H. Deverill dating back to 1890 with hikers posing in their dresses, dress shirts and ties, and stylish hats. On the back of the photo it read "'Ohi'alolo Waterfall," possibly giving another name to this beautiful plunge waterfall. With it being below Pu'u 'Ohi'a, the volcanic cone sitting on top of Tantalus, I sorta see where Ohi'alolo could be a fitting name.

Make sure to wear shoes with very good grip, and wear long sleeves or use bug repellant. Pack out what you pack in, and maybe even bring a garbage bag to collect waste that flows down Kanealole Stream on your way out. Let's always leave these amazing spots as good or better than we found them.

Miles and Directions

0.0 Start at the parking lot for the Hawai'i Nature Center.

0.27 Pass between the Hawai'i Nature Center and the restrooms to reach the trailhead just across the bridge.

0.38 Turn left to stay on the Kanealole Trail.

1.1 Turn right down an obscure trail to a concrete dam. Cross the dam and hike upstream/left on the unmaintained trail.

1.31 Arrive at Makiki Valley Falls. Enjoy the falls before retracing your steps.

2.62 Arrive back at the parking lot.

35 Manoa Falls

In the very back of Manoa Valley is the most popular waterfall on Oʻahu, and likely the most visited waterfall in all of Hawaiʻi: Manoa Falls. Hike up a recently renovated trail along Waihi Stream for about a mile to enjoy the light pouring through a break in the forest canopy onto a majestic 150-foot waterfall.

Height of falls: 150 feet
Type of falls: Plunge
Start: Paradise Park
Distance: 1.86 miles out and back
Difficulty: Easy
Hiking time: 1 to 1.5 hours (depending on how long you stay at the falls)
Elevation change: 450 feet
Trail surface: Wide rocky path
Seasons/schedule: Accessible year-round. Paradise Park is open daily from 9 a.m. to 6 p.m. You can go earlier or later by hiking in from the neighborhood.
Fees and permits: None to hike, but there is a fee to park in the Paradise Park parking lot.
Land status: Round Top Forest Reserve
Nearest town: Honolulu
Other trail users: Trail runners and waterfall photographers
Canine compatibility: Yes
Water availability: Indoor facilities and water hoses at the trailhead

Finding the trailhead: Approximately 6 miles from Honolulu, at the very end of Manoa Road, find Paradise Park and the Manoa Falls trailhead. Continue straight, even after the road narrows, to arrive at Paradise Park. Pay for parking (or park in the neighborhood to avoid the parking fee) and hike up the road from the parking lot, proceeding onto the well-marked Manoa Falls Trail. Pass on the left side of the gate to start the hike. Trailhead GPS: N21° 19.877', W157° 47.994'; Falls GPS: N21° 20.511', W157° 47.886'

The Hike

Hike up the valley road from Paradise Park, and check out the very informative trailhead signage at the large Manoa Falls Trail sign. Read about the species found in Manoa Valley and make note of the trail system the Manoa Falls Trail is a part of before starting your hike just to the left of the green gate.

Notice the expansive openness of this section of forest where the canopy of massive Albizia trees and the thick vines keep the rest of the jungle's growth stunted. Listen for the tropical birds that came to live here after the Paradise Park bird shows stopped performing years ago.

Pass through a container trailer and cross Waihi Stream at 0.23 mile. The trail turns left, continuing up the stream. It is a well-graveled, wide trail through a tropical rainforest of massive ferns, 20-foot-tall ginger, and towering trees. Continue through a forest of hau trees, banyan trees, and huge Albizia trees growing all along, and even in the middle of, the trail. Admire the girth of the huge Albizia trunks. Continue on to a quiet place to relax on a bench in a palm forest under banyan trees at 0.7 mile

Top: Start of the trail
Bottom: Hidden on the back of the trailhead signage

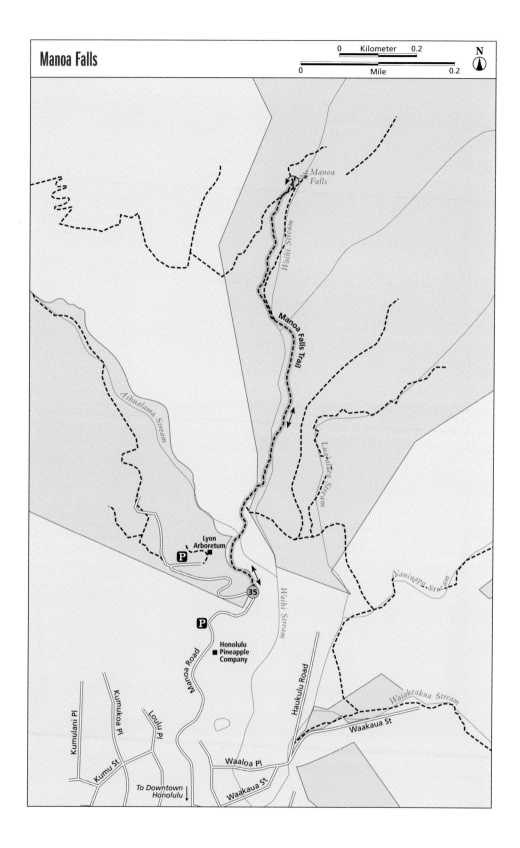

Manoa Falls

| 0 | Kilometer | 0.2 |
| 0 | Mile | 0.2 |

N

Manoa Falls

Waihi Stream

Manoa Falls Trail

Aihualama Stream

Luaalaea Stream

Naniuapa Stream

Lyon
Arboretum

P

35

P

Waihi Stream

Honolulu
Pineapple
Company

Manoa Road

Haukulu Road

Waiakeakua Stream

Waakaua St

Kumulani Pl

Kumukoa Pl

Loulu Pl

Kumu St

Waaloa Pl

Waakaua St

To Downtown
Honolulu

Please view from a safe distance.

Almost there

before beginning a slightly strenuous uphill section.

Take a second to look up to see the upper Manoa Falls as you climb the hill. Enjoy the mossy wall on your left and ti plants planted along the trail to your right. There are more benches to rest at and another informative sign at 0.8 mile. Listen for the white-rumped shama singing. Enjoy the bamboo, octopus trees, and wide variety of native and invasive ferns.

Pass the Aihualama Trail on your left at 0.9 mile and arrive at Manoa Falls at 0.93 mile. There is an observation deck and more benches to relax on while you take in the beauty of this place. The 150-foot-tall falls constantly flows into a small, shallow pool. Stay on the trail and back from the falls to avoid being hit by falling rocks, and stay out of the pool to avoid bacteria such as the one that causes leptospirosis.

This is the most popular waterfall trail in Hawai'i. It will be busy on weekends and holidays, so plan your trip accordingly. Watch for trail runners blasting through here during a weekend in January when this trail becomes part of the HURT 100 ultra-marathon. Be prepared for star sightings, as Manoa Falls is also a popular area for Hollywood productions. When hiking the trail for the writing of this book, the latest Aquaman movie was being filmed in the Albizia trees at the wide-open canopy area near the start of the trail!

Miles and Directions

0.0 Start at Paradise Park. Hike up the road to the Manoa Falls trailhead.

0.23 Cross Waihi Stream through a semitruck container. The trail then turns left up the stream.

0.7 Reach benches beside banyan trees before the last uphill climb.

0.9 Pass the Aihualama Trail on your left.

0.93 The trail ends at Manoa Falls. Enjoy the view before retracing your steps.

1.86 Arrive back at the trailhead.

36 Aihualama Falls (Lyon Arboretum)

Deep in the back of Manoa Valley, you can walk 0.9 mile of flat, very well marked and maintained trail to a lovely waterfall cascading into a small pool. You will encounter a wide variety of flora and fauna in this arboretum along your path to the approximately 30-foot-tall wet-weather waterfall.

Height of falls: 30 feet
Type of falls: Plunge
Start: Lyon Arboretum
Distance: 1.76 miles out and back
Difficulty: Easy
Hiking time: About 1 hour (depending on how much time you spend visiting the arboretum's gardens)
Elevation change: 260 feet
Trail surface: Wide paved path with a few dirt side trails through various gardens
Seasons/schedule: Accessible year-round. The arboretum is open 9 a.m. to 3 p.m. Monday through Friday.

Fees and permits: None, but donation appreciated
Land status: State of Hawai'i / University of Hawai'i
Nearest town: Honolulu
Other trail users: Nature bathers, bird-watchers, school groups, volunteers, and families
Canine compatibility: Yes
Water availability: Water fountain and rest-room at trailhead

Finding the trailhead: Approximately 6 miles from Honolulu, at the very end of Manoa Road, find Paradise Park and the Manoa Falls trailhead. Continue driving up the road, past the trailhead and park, to park at Lyon Arboretum. Let the parking attendant at Paradise Park know you are going to Lyon Arboretum and they will wave you by. Watch out for hikers as you drive up the road all the way to the gate for the Manoa Falls Trail, and then turn left into the gates for Lyon Arboretum. Continue all the way to the end of the road at the top of the hill, and park in the large parking lot. The welcome center and ticket counter are at the far end of the parking lot. Trailhead GPS: N21° 19.958', W157° 48.075'; Falls GPS: N21° 20.345', W157° 48.303'

The Hike

Although short and with a direct path along the main trail in Lyon Arboretum, I encourage you to meander throughout the expansive gardens and take in the beauty of this place. Matt Sorenson, Mary Muncher, Yoshi Akaha, and I started to the left of the visitor center, going behind it and down the hill into the gardens. We first visited a large Hawaiian section with lots of staple crops such as sugarcane, ulu (breadfruit), and kukui trees.

Since it is so close to Paradise Park, there are still some exotic birds flying around. A staff member at the old Paradise Park building (at the Manoa Falls trailhead parking

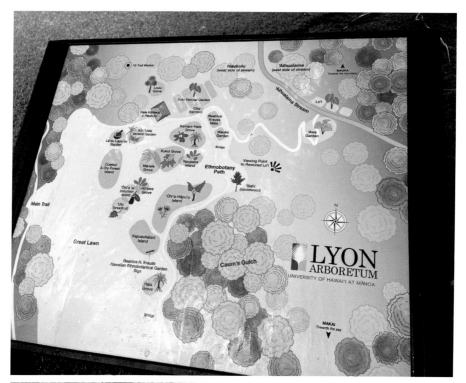

Top: Map of Lyon Arboretum
Bottom: Follow the signs.

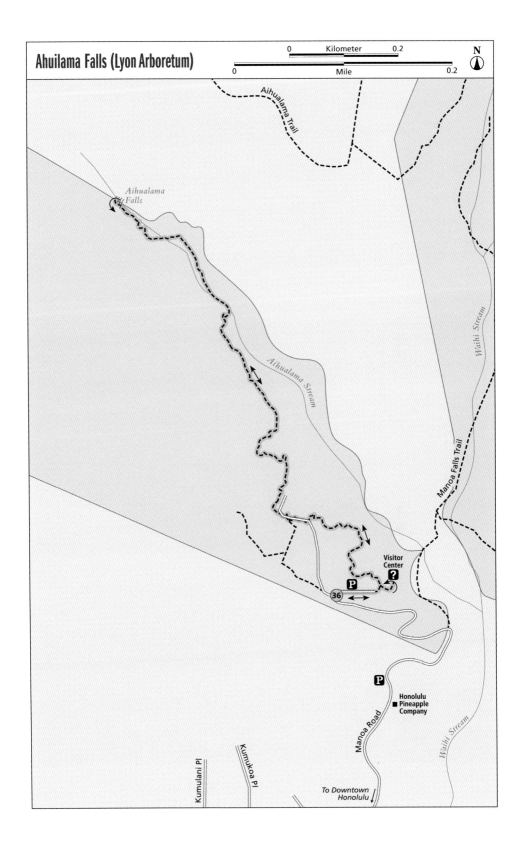

Ahuilama Falls (Lyon Arboretum)

0 Kilometer 0.2

0 Mile 0.2

N

Aihualama Trail

Aihualama
Falls

Waihi Stream

Aihualama Stream

Manoa Falls Trail

Visitor
Center

?

P

36

P

Honolulu
Pineapple
Company

Manoa Road

Waihi Stream

Kumulani Pl

Kumukoa Pl

To Downtown
Honolulu

The trail takes you right up to the falls.

area) said Paradise Park used to be an aviary. She said the birds had been set free years ago due to a major tropical storm.

The arboretum is named after Dr. Harold Lyon, who worked for the Hawai'i Sugar Planters Association. He helped reforest Hawai'i after the water crises of 1915, planting thousands of trees in these uplands and studying their growth.

We found another large Hawai'i section at 0.5 mile into our hike, this time mostly native trees. Stay on the main trail going forward. At 0.84 mile the trail turns left and divides. Continue to the left to see the falls. The trail then continues in front of the falls, allowing you to get very close. Now that you have reached Aihualama Falls, you can either go back the same way you came or take a different path back through Manoa Valley to your car. Make sure to bring some sunscreen and bug spray.

A day chasing waterfalls is a good day.

Miles and Directions

0.0 Start at the Lyon Arboretum parking lot. Check in at the visitor center, then hike to the left of the center.

0.1 Take the main trail toward Aihualama Falls.

0.84 Turn left where the trail divides.

0.9 The trail ends at Aihualama Falls. Enjoy the views before retracing your steps or continuing on to enjoy the various gardens.

1.8 Arrive back at the trailhead.

37 Queen's Bath

In the far-back eastern end of Manoa Valley is a trail system leading to lookouts and waterfalls. Start up the Pu'u Pia Trail and cross over to the Seven Bridges Trail to find a clear pool below a couple of nice waterfalls.

Height of falls: 10 feet and 20 feet
Type of falls: Fan and punchbowl
Start: Corner of Alani Road and Woodlawn Drive
Distance: 1.8 miles out and back
Difficulty: Moderate due to a short but very steep and muddy climb down from the Pu'u Pia Trail
Hiking time: 1.5 to 2 hours (depending on how long you stay at the pool)
Elevation change: 516 feet

Trail surface: Pavement to begin, then slick roots, mud, and rocks
Seasons/schedule: Accessible year-round
Fees and permits: None
Land status: State of Hawai'i
Nearest town: Honolulu
Other trail users: Fruit foragers and homeless people
Canine compatibility: Yes
Water availability: Stream water at the falls, which must be purified due to the risk of leptospirosis throughout the Hawai'i islands

Finding the trailhead: Approximately 6 miles from Honolulu, on the east side of Manoa Valley, follow E. Manoa Road to turn right onto Woodlawn Drive. The trailhead is at the corner of Woodlawn Drive and Alani Road. Park on the roadside and walk to the corner of Alani and Woodlawn. The trail is marked with a brown Nā Ala Hele sign with yellow lettering. Walk up the driveway to the left of the sign to start the hike. Trailhead GPS: N21° 19.232', W157° 47.843'; Falls GPS: N21° 19.696', W157° 47.416'

The Hike

Walk along the black pavement to the left of the Nā Ala Hele sign for the Pu'u Pia and Kolowalu Trails. It feels as though you are walking along a driveway at first, but the pavement ends after 300 feet and you cross a chain gate into a forest reserve. Walk up the dirt and gravel road into the woods.

The trail splits in 0.2 mile and you stay left on Pu'u Pia Trail. Continue up the rooted trail through a rainforest, which certainly can get muddy. Enjoy the super-dense vegetation and very thick tree roots as you climb the hill.

The trail flattens out at 0.73 mile. Look for an obscure trail down to your right, and go down the unmarked trail at 0.75 mile. (Just a little bit farther on the main trail takes you to Pu'u Pia and its 360-degree views of Manoa Valley.) Use caution climbing down this super-steep and slick muddy section.

Top: Queens Pool on a rainy day ▶
Bottom: A hidden gem

Meet another trail at 0.82 mile and turn right into the thicket of fan palm trees. The hike continues uphill to the right, but make sure to look back and make a mental note of how the trail looks for your return. You may even want to take a picture or be using a GPS device so you can find your way back to this steep section.

Hike the muddy path up for just a few hundred feet to a small falls with a wide pipe over the top of it at 0.88 mile. The waterfall pours into a nice pool that is typically crystal clear and refreshingly cold. Take in your surroundings, noticing what appears to be an old mine shaft on the far side of the falls. This is an old water irrigation tunnel from the days when Hawai'i was known for its sugar plantations.

Start on the Pu'u Pia Trail.

So clear!

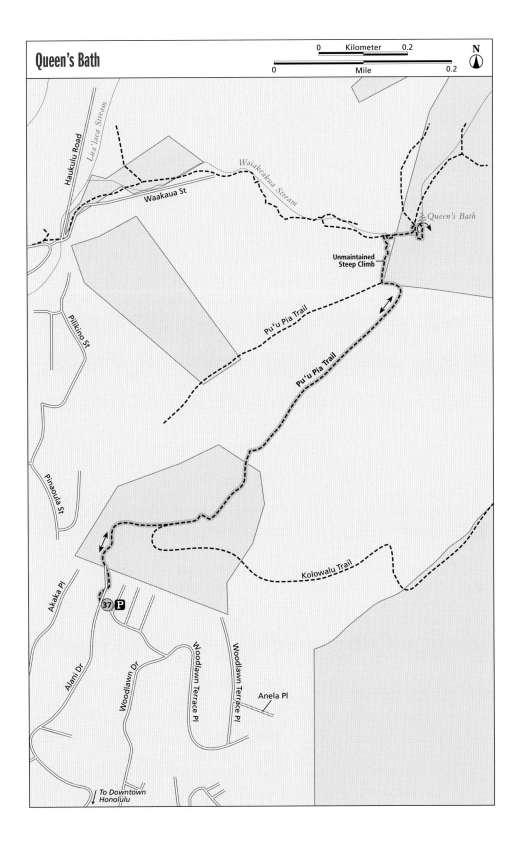

0   Kilometer   0.2

0   Mile   0.2

N

Haukulu Road

Lua 'Iaea Stream

Waiakeakua Stream

Waakaua St

Queen's Bath

Unmaintained
Steep Climb

Pilikino St

Pu'u Pia Trail

Pu'u Pia Trail

Pinaoula St

Kolowalu Trail

Akaka Pl

37 P

Alani Dr

Woodlawn Dr

Woodlawn Terrace Pl

Woodlawn Terrace Pl

Anela Pl

To Downtown
Honolulu

Small, but refreshing

Go up around the corner about 50 feet above the falls to find a second, more stunning falls that is approximately 20 feet tall. Be careful climbing around on the rocks in the streambed and watch out for flash floods. Remember that if the water turns brown, you should leave the streambed and seek higher ground.

Miles and Directions

0.0 Start to the left side of the Nā Ala Hele trail signs for the Kolowalu and Puʻu Pia Trails.

300 ft. Cross a chain gate where the trail changes from blacktop to gravel and dirt.

0.2 Stay left to remain on the Puʻu Pia Trail.

0.75 Turn right down a muddy, obscure trail.

0.82 Turn right at the trail intersection in the fan palms.

0.88 Arrive at Queen's Bath. Enjoy the two waterfalls and small plunge pool before retracing your steps.

1.76 Arrive back at the trailhead.

38 Manoa Cliff Overlook

From high above Honolulu and at the top of the Tantalus area, you can walk a short 0.87 mile of very well marked but slightly unmaintained trail to a dramatic overlook of Manoa Valley and three large waterfalls. Take in the view across the Nuʻuanu Saddle all the way to the windward side and the ocean.

Height of falls: Three or more falls, hundreds of feet each
Type of falls: Plunge
Start: Manoa Cliff trailhead on Round Top Drive
Distance: 1.78 miles out and back
Difficulty: Easy
Hiking time: About 1.5 hours (depending on how long you stay at the overlook and how fast you hike/run)
Elevation change: 317 feet

Trail surface: Wide dirt (oftentimes muddy because you're in a rainforest) path with a few rocky and narrow spots to be careful on while traversing
Seasons/schedule: Accessible year-round
Fees and permits: None
Land status: Mostly State of Hawaiʻi
Nearest town: Honolulu
Other trail users: Fruit foragers
Canine compatibility: Yes
Water availability: None

Finding the trailhead: Take either Round Top Drive or Tantalus Drive to the top of the Tantalus community. Park at the small roadside parking area (8 or 9 cars) on Round Top Drive at the Manoa Cliff Trail and Moleka Trail trailheads. Stay very quiet until you are on the trail, and make sure to be respectful of those living in this area. Trailhead GPS: N21° 19.533', W157° 48.726'; Overlook GPS: N21° 19.937', W157° 48.509'

The Hike

This is a beautiful hike along a gradually inclining trail on the cliff side of the majestic and sacred Manoa Valley. You will start below the heavy canopy of some very large trees. Cross the road from the parking lot and go into the dark forest at the Manoa Cliff trailhead. Be sure to wipe any dirt or alien plant spores off of your hiking boots at the trailhead brushes.

Right away you will be swept into whimsical treetops and open forest views. Look to your right at 0.13 mile to see a large blue marble tree with its high open crown and thin buttress roots at the base. Admire the beauty of a multilayer forest as you go up a few switchbacks at 0.2 mile into your hike.

Summit into thick strawberry guava at 0.28 mile. Embrace the mud at 0.3 mile, as there will be plenty more of it. You next traverse down six really big steps at 0.32 mile. After going down three switchbacks, you will find yourself on an open trail for what seems to be miles.

Take in the sweeping views at the many openings in the strawberry guava that dominates the trail sides. Look out and up for an old chimney at 0.48 mile. A view

Trail treats!

A relaxing spot

from Google Earth shows there are lots of homes up there, and this could likely be the remnants of one in that neighborhood. Either way, they probably have stunning views!

Pay attention to the slick trail, but be sure to stop and look around often. There are so many sights such as the view down Manoa Valley to see Diamond Head and the Pacific Ocean at 0.86 mile, native white hibiscus, ti plants, ie'ie, and so much more. There's no need to rush now, as the bench and view are just around the next corner.

Arriving at your destination at 0.89 mile in, you will see a tall bench overlooking sweeping views of Manoa Valley and three waterfalls: Manoa Falls, Kahuwai'iki Falls, and Lua'alaea Falls. As I sit on the bench I spy Pu'u 'Ohi'a behind me, the Nu'uanu Saddle and the Ko'olau Summit as they form the distant ridge above Pauoa Flats. Continuing right I see Konahuanui I and Konahuanui II (the highest peaks in the Ko'olau Mountain range at 3,150 feet and 3,050 feet, respectively), Manoa Saddle, Mount Olympus (2,486 feet tall), Ka'au Crater's summit, Wa'ahila Ridge running down from Mount Olympus, and the Lyon Arboretum below me. Native white hibiscus, flame red o'hia le'hua, fragrant white ginger, octopus trees, and ti plants surround me. This is a special place. Enjoy the trade winds blowing through the saddles and songbirds like the white-rumped shama singing to each other and you. Be immersed in the forest.

You can either turn back here for a 1.78-mile out-and-back or continue on to a variety of trails and adventures. The HURT 100 travels this trail five times in its five 20-mile loops. Competitors run for up to 36 hours, getting lapped by the sun as they try to survive this treacherous terrain for 100 miles! Manoa Falls is down the steep

So many canyons

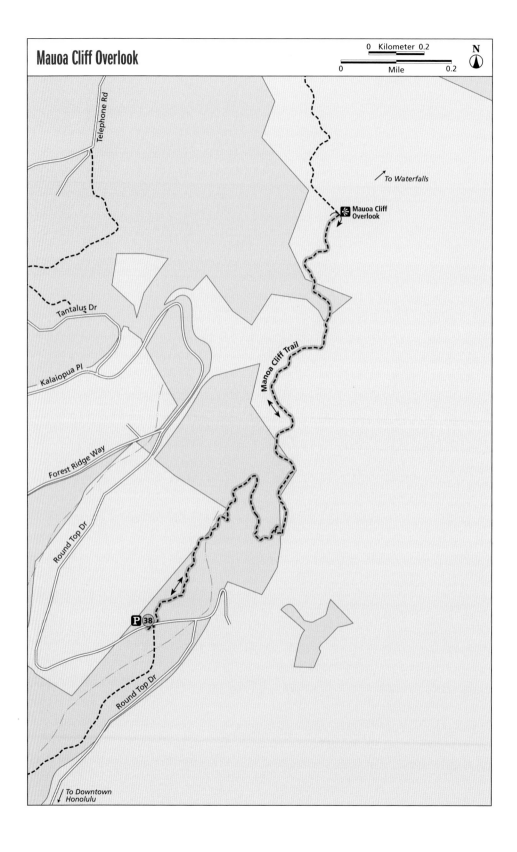

Mauoa Cliff Overlook

0   Kilometer 0.2

0   Mile   0.2

N

Telephone Rd

To Waterfalls

Mauoa Cliff
Overlook

Tantalus Dr

Manoa Cliff Trail

Kalaiopua Pl

Forest Ridge Way

Round Top Dr

P 38

Round Top Dr

To Downtown
Honolulu

Aihualama Trail, Jackass Ginger is down the steep Nuʻuanu Trail, Konahuanui is up the treacherous Pauoa Flats Trail, or you can make a fun 4.5-mile loop by crossing over to the Kalawahine Trail, going across Tantalus Road and down the Nahuina Trail to the Makiki Valley Trail, turning back left onto the Moleka Trail, and ending up back at the parking lot. Know your ability and plan your trip with the understanding you will need to be back before dark.

Miles and Directions

0.0 From the parking lot, cross the road and follow the Manoa Cliff Trail.

0.89 Arrive at a bench and an overlook of Manoa Valley. Look down into Manoa Valley to see up to three large waterfalls in the canyons across from you. Enjoy the views before retracing your steps.

1.78 Arrive back at the trailhead.

Focus to see the waterfalls flowing.

39 Waimano Falls

Hike along a ridgeline and down Cardiac Hill to find three waterfalls and three great pools for swimming.

Height of falls: Approximately 45 feet
Type of falls: Tier and plunge
Start: Manana trailhead at the end of Komo Mai Drive
Distance: 2.88 miles out and back
Difficulty: Difficult
Hiking time: 3 to 4 hours (depending on how long you stay at the pools)
Elevation change: 164 feet
Trail surface: Paved utility road before muddy, rooted, and rocky slick trail, then rock-climbing down very large steps and slick handholds

Seasons/schedule: Accessible year-round
Fees and permits: None
Land status: Ewa Forest Reserve
Nearest town: Aiea, the only city in America that doesn't have a consonant in its name
Other trail users: Pig hunters
Canine compatibility: Yes
Water availability: Stream water at the falls, which must be purified due to the risk of leptospirosis throughout the Hawai'i islands. *Do not swim if the water is not flowing!*

Finding the trailhead: From Pearl City, take Waimano Home Road to Komo Mai Drive. Park along the road at the end of Komo Mai Drive. Stay very quiet until you are on the trail, and make sure to be respectful to people living near the trailhead. Walk to the end of Komo Mai Drive, where there is a cul-de-sac, then continue on straight past the green gate, on its right. Trailhead GPS: N21° 25.800', W157° 56.242'; Falls GPS: N21° 25.929, W157° 55.245'

The Hike

This route is difficult and should only be attempted by expert hikers. Enter to the right of the green gate at the end of Komo Mai Drive. Follow the old roadbed, a utility road for power lines and a water tank. You will see mostly ironwood trees along the trail.

Pass under power lines at 0.2 mile, then continue on the road. Go under more high-voltage lines at 0.33 mile. Continue along the trail, now at the top of the ridge with views on both sides. Enjoy the breeze and views of canyons and diverse flora including Philippine ground orchids, koa trees, Cook pines, eucalyptus, mango trees, and uluhe ferns.

The paved road ends at a water tower surrounded by a fence with razor wire on top at 0.44 mile. Continue straight and stay on the wide trail along the ridgetop for now. Go under one more set of power lines at 0.49 mile. Enjoy the sweeping views of the Waianae Mountains to the west, with Mount Kaala, the highest peak on O'ahu, on the northern end of them.

The trail continues straight into the forest and is much more shaded from here on. Go up a rooted section of trail in a eucalyptus forest at 0.56 mile. Stay left after

Enter past the green gate.

topping the hill. Enjoy the view into the valley on your right and then expansive views while you hike along the rolling trail. Stay on top of the ridge, being careful of some of the mudded areas, and enjoy another small lookout at 0.77 mile.

Turn right at the split in the trail at 0.85 mile. Go down, off of the Manana Trail, toward Waimano Falls and not up the 7-mile-long Manana Ridge to the Koʻolau Summit. The trail gets more muddy and rooted from here on out. Continue down to the right again at 0.87 mile. It will be slick in spots and you may even want to wear shoe spikes.

Continue down Cardiac Hill at 1.0 mile into your hike. You will be taking very large steps and using your whole body to traverse this section. After dropping down 200 feet in 0.1 mile, you find a stream crossing with even more mud at 1.11 miles. There are yellow guava and tons of strawberry guava here, and some ropes to help stabilize yourself as you scramble down the rocks. The real climbing starts at 1.2 miles and turns to legitimate rock-climbing at 1.26 miles.

You take a hard left at 1.26 miles. Make sure to watch for the turn at the bottom of the steep rocky section. Many people get lost here. The rough trail continues with high roots, low branches, slick rocks, and very high steps. You will start noticing even more mosquitoes as you get closer to the streambed.

Waimano Falls

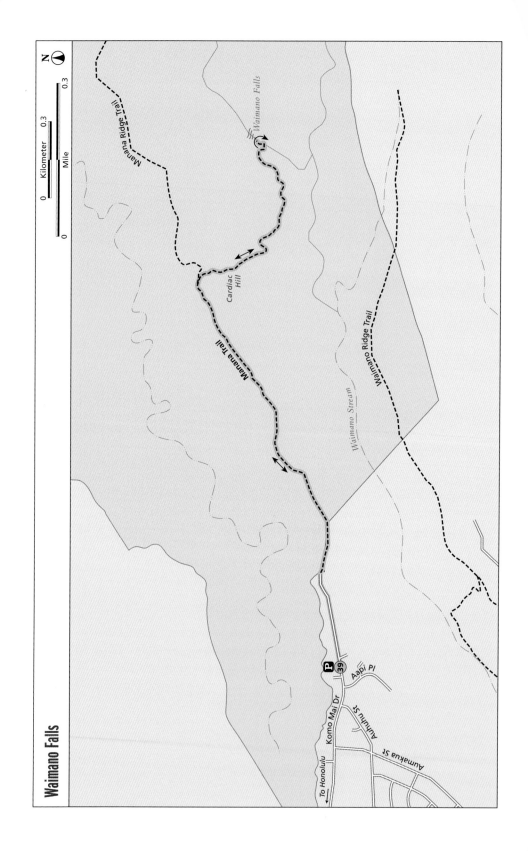

N

Kilometer
0   0.3

Mile
0   0.3

Manana Ridge Trail

Waimano Falls

Cardiac Hill

Manana Trail

Waimano Stream

Waimano Ridge Trail

To Honolulu

Komo Mai Dr

Aapi Pl

Aumakua St

Auhuhu St

P 39

Good flow

A murky water day

Turn left again at the split at 1.28 miles. There will be lots of strawberry guava, mud, and native ferns. Enjoy a nice, clear view of the canyon and stream below at 1.34 miles. The trail gets steep downhill again at 1.4 miles, as you climb down to see the pools and falls at 1.44 miles.

The largest falls, at approximately 40 to 50 feet tall, has a big shallow pool at the bottom. It flows into a smaller falls of approximately 5 feet tall that fills a hot-tub-size and chest-deep plunge pool. Then the second pool flows out to make another small falls with a larger plunge pool below it. There is a rope swing and many spots along the cliffs on both sides of the stream that people jump off into the pool. *Do not dive,* as the water is shallow. And only jump up to your skill level. Due to the risk of lepto-spirosis in stagnant water, *do not swim if the water is not flowing!*

When explaining my method of rating trails at the beginning of this book, I said that the waterfall will always be there whenever you are ready to return. I first visited Waimano Falls with a bunch of college kids out for summer break in 1999. My buddy Jeff Shaw's father was stationed at Pearl Harbor, and I was lucky enough to stay part of the summer in their big house.

Jeff and his brother took me in an old-school Volkswagen Beetle to the neighbor-hood trailhead, where we met up with their friends, hiked to the falls, and swam a bit. I was enamored with the place, calmed by the chill vibes Jeff's rock star brother and friends were putting out, and totally overwhelmed by the rugged climb down to the swimming holes complete with cliff jumps and rope swings. It was a very good day.

Unfortunately, I left the islands and headed back to school at the University of Tennessee without first getting directions to Waimano Falls. I completely forgot how we got there (maybe because it was hard to see out from my fetal position in the backseat of the VW Bug?), and I looked for the falls for years and years after that.

I asked Jeff where we went, and he suggested it might have been Maunawili Falls. I went there, but it wasn't it. There was no Cardiac Hill with myriad roots to climb down.

It took me until I was hiking with a Meetup group in 2014 to find Waimano Falls again! I knew as soon as I was climbing step by step, hand over hand down Cardiac Hill that I was in that oh-so-familiar place. I told my friends that I had been there before . . . in a previous life. I explained that we would end at a series of pools with waterfalls and cliff jumps. It all came flooding back to me. Since then I have been back to swim in Waimano's pools many, many times.

And on the issue of safety, I have turned around many times when I was running out of daylight, noticed the water level rising, or came upon a cliff I didn't feel comfortable climbing that day. When writing this book, I turned around twice due to potential flash floods. Like Waimano Falls, I didn't give up hope and I kept searching and preparing. Sure enough, fifteen years later the waterfall was still there.

Miles and Directions

0.0 Start by going straight past the green gate at the end of Komo Mai Drive to start the Manana Trail.

0.56 Stay left after topping the hill.

0.85 Turn right at the split to go down a contour trail on the way to Cardiac Hill.

1.26 Turn hard left at the bottom of the steep rocky section.

1.28 Turn left again at the split in the trail.

1.44 Climb down a very steep rock section to arrive at the falls and pools. Enjoy the three waterfalls and pools before retracing your steps.

2.88 Arrive back at the Manana trailhead.

40 Ho‘omaluhia

Just outside of Kaneohe is the large Ho‘omaluhia Botanical Garden with stunning views of the Ko‘olau Mountains across the Nu‘uanu Saddle, Pu‘u Lanihuli, the Kalihi Saddle, and Bowman. Relax on one of the great lawns, teach your kid to fish in the stocked pond, or just hammock or picnic for a bit while you study the wall, scanning for flowing water going down the thousand-foot-tall waterfall chutes above you.

Height of falls: Various falls dropping hundreds of feet
Type of falls: Tier and plunge
Start: Ho‘omaluhia Botanical Garden visitor center
Distance: Various hikes with different lengths. The most popular is hiking to the pond at 0.2 mile below the visitor center.
Difficulty: Easy
Hiking time: Depends on how long you stay at the gardens and how much you walk
Elevation change: Varies
Wheelchair accessible: Yes

Trail surface: Wide concrete and dirt paths
Seasons/schedule: Accessible year-round. Open 9 a.m. to 4 p.m. daily, except Christmas Day and New Year's Day.
Fees and permits: None
Land status: Ho‘omaluhia Botanical Garden
Nearest town: Kaneohe
Other trail users: Fruit foragers, Scouts, volunteers, and state employees
Canine compatibility: Yes
Water availability: Many water fountains and restrooms throughout the gardens

Finding the trailhead: Park at the Ho‘omaluhia Botanical Garden visitor center on left side of the road 1 mile up from the guard shack, and walk wherever you like while enjoying views of the waterfalls coming off of the Ko‘olau Mountains. Hike all over this beautiful garden while looking up to the mountains and counting the waterfalls. I once walked over 7 miles taking in the beauty of this place. Trailhead GPS: N21° 23.185', W157° 48.475'; Falls GPS: Multiple Falls

The Hike

I write this review while enjoying lunch at a picnic table beside the visitor center and peering into a massive waterfall chute. Today it is flowing a steady white flow, occasionally disappearing in spots when the wind blows it to the side. The tables appear new and clean, and I count eight of them from where I sit. Oh wait, now I see another falls even higher up! Although it is faint, it is majestic and seemingly disappears into the abyss that is the massive cliff face covered in octopus trees, moss, and ferns. On a good day there are many of these chutes full of flowing waterfalls. The hanging valleys off the side of Kalihi Saddle charge up with cold, clean mountain rain, then drop down the thousand-foot sea cliffs like manna from heaven.

Pay attention and you may see long-tailed tropic birds fluttering to their cliff-side caves and feeding their families the fish they just pulled out of Kaneohe Bay. Their long white tail looks as if it were a wand composing a grand symphony. The forest

A royal welcome

birds sing from the trees all around, while zebra doves and little brown birds hop through the grassy field that surrounds me. Sadly, I also hear the brakes of a semitruck coming off the mountain on Interstate H–3 and some loud mufflers from the Likelike Highway. But I can even escape those loud machines by adventuring onto the trails throughout the botanical gardens.

Feel free to walk, bike, or drive along the road deep into the gardens while gazing up at the layers upon layers of razor-sharp ridges capped by equally impressive features such as the witch's hat, door stop, two poles, Bowman, and Lanihuli. You can even see around the corner and into the Nu'uanu Saddle on the south side and almost to Haiku Stairs ("The Stairway to Heaven") on the north.

Wander around the various grassy fields and trails and you will see a variety of palms, banyans, bamboo, Albizia trees, flowers, ferns, fruit, and even lots of koi fish in the pond. Walk a short 0.2 mile down the hill from the visitor center to a large pond where you can fish. Follow the signs that say "To Lake" to the right of the visitor center. Stay on the paved zigzagging walkway through trees, palms, bamboo, and flowering plants from around the world.

The trail turns to gravel at 0.15 mile and opens into a large field overlooking the lake. Look back to see the cliffs of the Ko'olau Mountains pouring waterfalls high above you. There are restrooms here and a picnic pavilion. You'll see lots of families playing in the grassy fields, picnickers, and parents teaching their children how to fish while watching their faces light up with a smile when they land one.

Waterfalls pour off Puʻu Lanihuli.

Above: View from the visitor center picnic tables
Below: Look for the Nu'uanu and Kalihi Saddles.

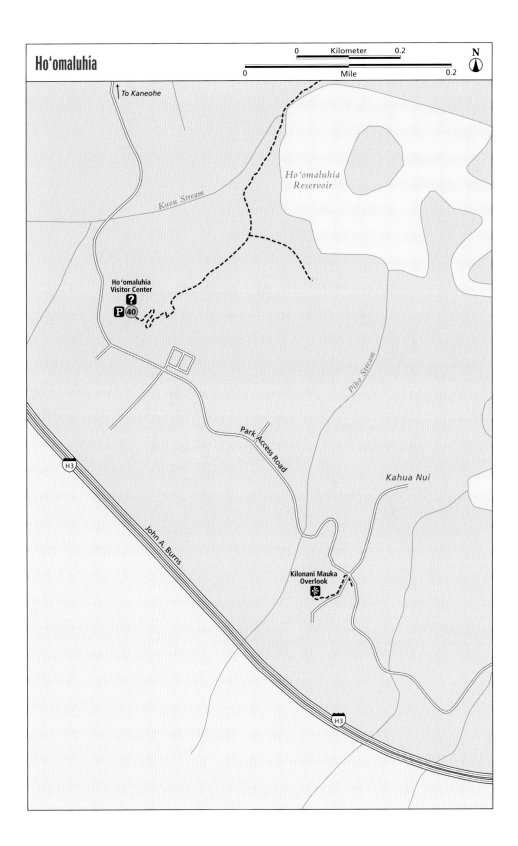

Ho'omaluhia

N

0   Kilometer   0.2

0   Mile   0.2

To Kaneohe

Ho'omaluhia
Reservoir

Kuou Stream

Ho'omaluhia
Visitor Center

P 40

Piho Stream

Park Access Road

Kahua Nui

H3

John A. Burns

Kilonani Mauka
Overlook

H3

A close look shows how massive the falls are.

Another great view is found at the Kilonani Mauka Overlook. Drive (or walk) past the visitor center and the Pa Launa and Kahua Kuou gardens. Look for the pull-off on your right after you go up the hard S-turn in the road. Park and walk up the steep concrete road (on the opposite side from the Kahua Lehua section) approximately 400 feet past the chain gate to a 360-degree view of the mountains and the ocean. There is a sign here explaining they do not allow drones or remote-controlled aircraft in this area.

You can rent spaces to overnight camp, from one person to a large group. Ask to see if they have any volunteering opportunities. It is certainly the kind of place I could spend a lot of days at. The serenity and beauty are quintessential Hawai'i.

Ho'omaluhia is one of five Honolulu Botanical Gardens. The others are Foster Botanical Garden, Lili'uokalani Botanical Garden, Wahiawa Botanical Garden, and Koko Crater Botanical Garden. The Lili'uokalani Botanical Garden even includes the soothing Waikahalulu Waterfall. Find their hours of operation and check them all out at www.honolulubotanicalgardens.com.

Miles and Directions

Wander throughout the large grounds of this tropical botanical garden while admiring the massive sea cliffs with cascading waterfalls high above. Hike to the Loko Waimaluhia fish pond or high Kilonani Mauka Overlook and look toward the Ko'olau Mountains to see many waterfalls.

Molokai Waterfalls

Molokai is as close to ancient Hawai'i as any island you can visit. The hustle and bustle of the other islands is not seen here. The overdevelopment of coastlines like Waikiki and Lahaina has never happened. The land has stayed natural for the most part, and so have the streams. Although the sugarcane industry was briefly established here, it never reached the mass scale of other islands, and Molokai didn't see as much of the diversion of streams and installation of irrigation ditches.

The bog at the top of Molokai, Pepe'opae, sits high atop the mountains in the Kamokou Preserve, at around 4,300 feet elevation. It houses numerous native plants and has been preserved by the Nature Conservancy through a conservation easement with Molokai Ranch, Ltd., since 1982. The preserve is full of native ferns, wildlife, and trees. It catches the moisture from the clouds and puts it into the ground to flow into streams that create beautiful waterfalls.

Some of the highest sea cliffs in the world are located on North Molokai. With these massive cliffs and ancient bog set atop them, it is the perfect combination for *huge* waterfalls. Sailors are blessed as they pass by the island with one of the most jaw-dropping scenes on the planet. The rains fall on the ridges high atop Moloakai's east side, flowing down from its highest peak, Kamakou at 4,961 feet, to create Waikolu Valley, Pelekunu Valley, Wailau Valley, and Halawa Valley. An untouched rainforest exists in each of these valleys, with flowing water so clean, the locals living there don't even filter or purify it.

41 Mo'oula Falls

True Hawai'i is revealed as you take a cultural tour with Greg Kawaimaka Solatorio and his father, Anakala Pilipo Solatorio, who both grew up in Halawa Valley. Listen to the history of the Hawaiian people as you journey to the back of Halawa Valley to the very tall and heavily flowing Mo'oula Falls with its huge pool to swim in.

Height of falls: 250 feet
Type of falls: Tier
Start: Halawa Park
Distance: 4.6 miles out and back
Difficulty: Moderate
Hiking time: 4 to 6 hours (depending on the length of the tour and how long you stay at the pool)
Elevation change: 300 feet
Trail surface: Dirt and rocks
Seasons/schedule: Accessible year-round. Closed on Sunday and certain other days when private tours are occurring. Visit http://halawa-valleymolokai.com for tour availability.
Fees and permits: Tour fee
Land status: Private land
Nearest town: Kaunakakai
Other trail users: None
Canine compatibility: No, except for service dogs
Water availability: Water in the stream only, which must be purified before drinking due to the risk of leptospirosis

Finding the trailhead: From Kaunakakai, take Kamehameha V Highway / HI 450 east 28 miles all the way to the end of the road. Park at Halawa Park. Your tour guide will meet you here. Trailhead GPS: N21° 09.444', W156° 44.288'; Falls GPS: N21° 09.257', W156° 45.871'

The Hike

Meet Greg at Halawa Park to start your tour. The tours usually start around 9 or 9:30 a.m. If there has been a heavy rain the night before, or if one is forecasted that day, you may have to postpone the hike due to the risk of flash flooding. We drove to Halawa Park one morning only to have to come back the next day. Greg was great and offered to take us to his home for a cultural tour that day or give a refund if we didn't have the time to come back. We had an extra day, so we came back and hiked it the next day.

Walk up the road from Halawa Park away from Halawa Beach. Halawa was a taro farming community that was consumed by a 36-foot-tall tsunami wave in 1946. On your left just after leaving Halawa Park you can still see some of the damage left behind as you pass the old Halawa Congregational Church built in 1852, which was destroyed by the tidal wave. Turn right onto a dirt road at 450 feet into your hike to head toward Greg's home and the trail to the falls. You are immediately transported into a rainforest with philodendron vines hanging from large mango trees.

Make sure you mind the No Trespassing signs. Stop to announce your arrival into the valley at the gate at 0.17 mile into your hike. Greg will blow a large conch shell for the valley residents to know the tour is coming. Since we are so far from civilization and out of cell phone reception deep in Halawa Valley, the "shell phone" is the only phone that works here.

Beside your path at 0.2 mile you will notice ancient walls that were once part of the Halawa Valley community and lots of banana trees. Enjoy the ginger and red hibiscus flowers that litter your path. An ancient irrigation ditch lies dry along the right side of the roadbed.

You will enter a large clearing at 0.42 mile with a view of the falls and some of the residences of the valley. Greg may show you his home at 0.48 mile and even offer you some of the fruits he has picked that morning. The trail to Mo'oula Falls starts right out of his home and behind the Hale Ike O Halawa fruit stand.

You are immediately transported back to ancient Hawai'i as you step through the fencing and into the *loi* terraces maintained by Greg and his family. See how the taro

Meet your guide here.

Moʻoula Falls

Look for the upper tiers as you approach the falls.

plants and the gardens that surround them were cultivated to sustain the people of the valley. Follow along, listening closely to the tales of the approximately 5,000 residents who once called this valley home.

The first stream crossing occurs at 0.62 mile. Be prepared to wade through the stream, as the rocks are too slick to hop across. Climb up the hill after crossing the stream to the trail below the rock wall, following it to the right. Climb old farming terraces and across a flowing irrigation ditch at 0.66 mile. Watch your step across this narrow ditch and make sure to step between the slick rocks, not on top of them, for the best footing.

Orange-colored Brazilian cherries litter your path as you continue along the trail. You next see a large hala tree on your right at 0.87 mile. Hala is a native Hawaiian plant with a variety of uses. Greg explained how male hala trees have flowers, while females have the seed pods. I've often seen these seed pods, which look almost like pineapples when they are hanging from the tree and pieces of candy corn when they fall and bust open.

Next you pass through a hau tunnel with their yellow flowers littering the ground. Hau is a cousin to the hibiscus, which you can see in the similarity of their flowers. Ancient Hawaiians used to rub the hau sticks together to create fire and used the hau and hala fibers to make strong ropes. Not much was ever wasted, and many uses came from each plant, demonstrating the ingenuity of the Hawaiian people.

The trail is covered with kukui nuts at 0.94 mile into your hike and there are more Brazilian cherry trees. Watch your step as the trail makes a slight climb up a path of boulders at 1.17 miles. Then pass a huge monkey pod tree on your left with many bird's nest ferns growing on its branches at 1.44 miles into the hike. Next you will find three large mango trees on your left, with various stone walls going different directions.

At 1.72 miles you will see even more stone walls, which were the living areas of the people of the Halawa *ahupua'a*. Their fields were all along the flat space below the trail and they lived above it. The trail through here is called the Hana Trail, which translates to the "working trail." Workers would travel this trail daily, harvesting the crops and bringing the fish up from the bay below.

You will see a huge ylang ylang tree at 1.8 miles, with its fruit littering the trail. *Do not eat it!* There is a nice pool in the stream at 1.9 miles as the trail rejoins the stream. Pass through large palm leaves and feel the cool breeze on this easy section of trail. Be extra respectful at 2.0 miles, as you find a very large Heiau with its seven levels leading up to the very large sacrificial alter stone.

Turn right after the alter and stay on the flatland by the river as you near the falls. The trail rejoins the stream with a nice pool at 2.16 miles before your second stream crossing at 2.2 miles into your hike. The trail continues, rock-hopping its way to the falls and large pool at 2.3 miles.

Mo'oula Falls

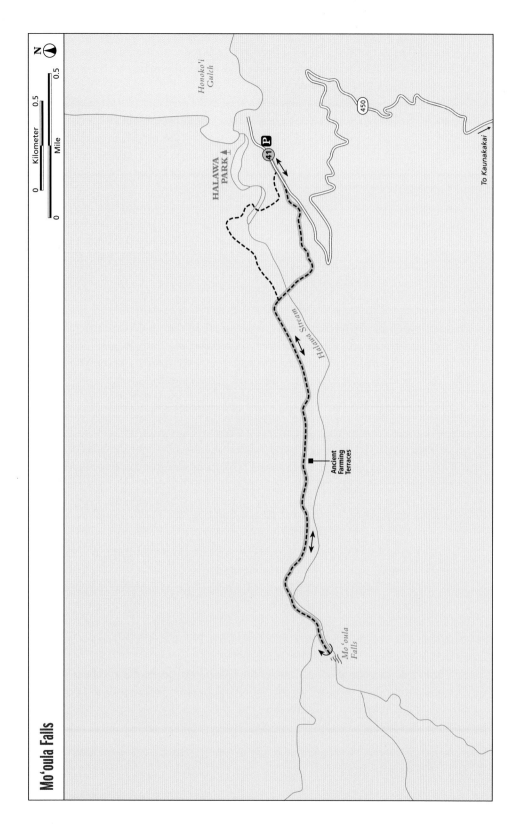

Homoko'i
Gulch

HALAWA
PARK

P

41

Halawa Stream

To Kaunakakai

450

Ancient
Farming
Terraces

Mo'oula
Falls

N

Kilometer
0   0.5

0   0.5
Mile

Miles and Directions

0.0 Start at Halawa Park.

0.1 Turn right onto the road to Greg's house.

0.48 The trail turns right at Hale Ike O Halawa and goes down through *loi* terraces.

0.62 Reach the first Halawa Stream crossing.

2.2 Come to the second crossing over Halawa Stream.

2.3 The trail ends at Mo'oula Falls. Enjoy the falls and pool before retracing your steps.

4.6 Arrive back at the trailhead.

Additional Information

At Halawa Park we met Greg and his father, Pilipo. Pilipo grew up in Halawa Valley and witnessed firsthand the transition of Hawai'i into statehood. His forefathers handed down the stories of their generations to him as the cultural practitioner of the family. In ancient Hawai'i there were no books or written records of events, so they passed down their tribal and familial stories through chants, songs, and stories. Meeting someone like Pilipo is like finding a link to pre-historical times. One can learn a lot from the ways of old, and we were blessed to be learning from one of the purveyors of history.

Greg is one of Pilipo's six children. He currently resides in Halawa Valley after living for a while in Honolulu. He leads cultural tours daily and is often booked for many months or even a year out, so make sure to book your tour early! Greg shows that through respect and love, the spirit of Hawai'i has survived for over a thousand years. Ancient ways of sustainable living are practiced daily, with the *'aina* providing much of the meat, produce, water, and supplies necessary to live in this remote place. Greg leads hunting tours to harvest and manage the axis deer, blackbuck antelope, turkey, and other animals that have been introduced over the years.

Listen to how the Hawaiian islands were divided into *ahupua'as* under the rule of the chiefdom system before King Kamehameha united the islands under one system. Hear about how wave after wave of Polynesians came with their cultures, beliefs, and political systems. Find out about how Greg led archeologists to a fire pit with relics dating back to AD 650, demonstrating the history of Hawai'i is way longer than many previously expected. Hear how *aloha* means "love" more than it means "hello" or "good-bye." And feel the love of the Hawaiian people wanting to share their culture and ways of living so that we may all survive in unity with the land. Molokai is different, and how lucky we are that it has stayed that way.

Visit http://halawavalleymolokai.com for fees and additional information. Swimming is free, but make sure to listen to Guide Greg when he tells you when and where it is safe to swim. There are no changing rooms at the falls.

There are no food and beverage concession stands in Halawa Valley, so make sure to gear up in town or stop at one of the shops along Kamehameha V Highway before descending the road into the valley.

Appendix A: Contacts

Backpacking and Camping Permits

Nā Ala Hele–Hawai'i's Trail and Access Program
https://hawaiitrails.hawaii.gov/trails
Up-to-date information about the open status of Hawai'i state trails. Less detailed trail descriptions.

Hawai'i Department of Land and Natural Resources (DLNR), Department of Forestry and Wildlife (DOFAW)
http://hawaii.gov/dlnr/dofaw

In addition to DOFAW permits, permits from other divisions within the DLNR or from outside agencies may be required. It is the individual's sole responsibility to ensure that all applicable permits are held prior to commencement of regulated activities.

Examples of regulated activities include:

1. Activities within a state forest reserve (including collection, commercial harvest, camping, and access for research)
2. Camping permits
3. Commercial hiking permits
4. Hunting licenses, hunt applications, and special hunt permit applications

When in doubt, check DOFAW's website.

Other permitting: To perform various activities such as events, scientific collection of plants and animals, or commercial activities within a Hawai'i state forest reserve, you must obtain a Special Use Permit. Because the Special Use Permit covers a broad range of activities, the process and time frame varies considerably depending on the proposed activity. Call or submit a request in writing describing the nature of your proposed activity, location, time frames, and other associated information to the appropriate branch office:

Hawai'i Branch Office
19 E. Kawali Street
Hilo, HI 96720
(808) 974-4221

Maui Nui Branch Office
54 S. High Street
Wailuku, HI 96793
(808) 984-8100

Kaua'i Branch Office
3060 Elwa Street, Room 306
Lihue, HI 96766
(808) 274-3433

O'ahu Branch Office
2135 Makiki Heights Drive
Honolulu, HI 96822
(808) 973-9778

Hiking and Backpacking Gear

Uloha–Hawai'i's Hiking Store
"Get in here to get out there."
515 Ward Avenue
Honolulu, HI 96814
(909) 475-7450
Ulohamail@gmail.com
www.uloha.com

Appendix B: Additional Reading

Ball, Stuart, Jr. *The Backpackers Guide to the Hawai'i*. Honolulu: University of Hawai'i Press, 1996.

———. *The Hikers Guide to the Hawaiian Islands*, updated and expanded. Honolulu University of Hawai'i Press, 2018.

———. *The Hikers Guide to O'ahu*, updated and expanded. Honolulu: University of Hawai'i Press, 2013.

———. *Native Paths to Volunteer Trails: Hiking and Trail Building on O'ahu*. Honolulu University of Hawai'i Press, 2012.

McMahon, Richard. *Camping Hawai'i*. Honolulu: University of Hawai'i Press, 1997.

Hike Index

THE TEN ESSENTIALS OF HIKING

American Hiking Society

American Hiking Society recommends you pack the "Ten Essentials" every time you head out for a hike. Whether you plan to be gone for a couple of hours or several months, make sure to pack these items. Become familiar with these items and know how to use them. Learn more at **AmericanHiking.org/hiking-resources**

1. Appropriate Footwear

6. Safety Items (light, fire, and a whistle)

2. Navigation

7. First Aid Kit

3. Water (and a way to purify it)

8. Knife or Multi-Tool

4. Food

9. Sun Protection

5. Rain Gear & Dry-Fast Layers

10. Shelter

PROTECT THE PLACES YOU LOVE TO HIKE

Become a member today and take $5 off an annual membership using the code **Falcon5**.

AmericanHiking.org/join

American Hiking Society is the only national nonprofit organization dedicated to empowering all to enjoy, share, and preserve the hiking experience.